Corrupt Judge, Corrupt Trial

Michael M. Ceperich

Note for Librarians: A cataloguing record for this book is available from Library and Archives Canada at www.collectionscanada.ca/amicus/index-e.html
ISBN 1-4251-1333-8

Offices in Canada, USA, Ireland and UK

Book sales for North America and international:
Trafford Publishing, 6E–2333 Government St.,
Victoria, BC V8T 4P4 CANADA
phone 250 383 6864 (toll-free 1 888 232 4444)
fax 250 383 6804; email to orders@trafford.com
Book sales in Europe:
Trafford Publishing (UK) Limited, 9 Park End Street, 2nd Floor
Oxford, UK OX1 1HH UNITED KINGDOM
phone 44 (0)1865 722 113 (local rate 0845 230 9601)
facsimile 44 (0)1865 722 868; info.uk@trafford.com
Order online at:
trafford.com/06-3092

10 9 8 7 6 5 4 3 2 1

To my dear wife Elizabeth ...

... all my love, always.

Corrupt Judge, Corrupt Trial

Contents

Corrupt Judge, Corrupt Trial

1
My Purpose

When I began this writing, I was 82 years old and my wife was 79. I did so in order to tell how we had been taken advantage of by so-called friends, attorneys and possibly even judges. We thought always that the justice system would be there to protect us from harm, but we were sorely mistaken.

I took to writing this book to share with you the truth about how our Mobile Home Park was stolen from us, how we got it back, and how the whole stress-filled experience has changed our lives forever. And I share with you my personal tragedy.

In writing this book I am making my appeal, since my attorneys will not, or at least have not to this point. I feel we have been used and abused by both individuals and our justice system.

You will see in this true story that Paolo Sessa took advantage of the fact that my wife and I were senior citizens, and he sought out attorneys and judges to help him. Paolo Sessa used our trust in people and our ignorance of real estate to cheat us out of approximately $400,000.

Paolo Sessa did not do this over a period of weeks or months, but over a period of very well-planned and thought out years, for two years prior to our sale to him of the Ramona Mobile Home Park (RMHP) and for almost four more years while he was the "owner" of the Park.

After those four years, I got back a neglected piece of property that needed major repair, a new loan that I had to take out to pay off the property that I previously owned outright, and an extremely bad taste in my mouth about our justice system.

I now owe on the new loan for the Park, I owe attorney's fees, and I still have significant repairs to make to the RMHP.

Moreover and most importantly, my wife has since passed away, and I am overcome with grief, not only at her passing, but also because our last years together were marred by the constant and incessant turmoil surrounding Sessa, our last attorney, Kenneth Zalud, and the numerous court appearances and depositions we were both subjected to.

I will not ever be able to forget the sadness that seemed to fill her last days, the strained and tearful look on her face as she lay in bed. Among her last words were these: "Corrupt judge...corrupt trial." Her last thoughts were not of the pleasant life we shared in the back country of northeast San Diego County, but of our recent ordeal with the justice system.

For two years the Sessas courted us until we sold them our Mobile Home Park. For two years after that we watched as they slowly dismantled the Park and drove a wedge of distrust between them and us. Indeed, like a row dominoes, the pillars on which we had based our life together crumbled. And for the rest of her life we grappled with the justice system.

This was not how I saw us passing our last days. This was not what I would have wanted my dear wife, my life's companion, to have on her mind on her death bed. This should not have happened to us. Her very last words should not have been, "Cruel world...I go in peace."

I am now 84 years old and alone in the world. I don't know if I'll find the energy to continue to pursue justice through the courts, but I will have the satisfaction of knowing that I got the truth out there. What should be done with this truth is something I'm less and less sure of as time passes.

And at this point recovering the money that was stolen from me seems less important than setting all this down in print.

But I would do anything to have my life back with Elizabeth.

Ramona Mobile Home Park

2
Our Mobile Home Park

In 1969, My wife and I purchased the Ramona Mobile Home Park as an investment toward our retirement. We had already fallen in love with the back country of northeast San Diego County, so we could think of no better place to retire. Not only has the RMHP provided us with a way to make a living, but also we have ourselves been tenants since 1972.

We have also been able to make many good friends and even been able to help a few people who had nowhere else to turn, and that has been especially gratifying. People from all over the country have taken up residence in our Mobile Home Park. It has been a peaceful, beautiful place to call home.

As the years went by, many changes took place in the Ramona Valley. In the eighties, many developers became aggressively interested in placing Ramona on the map. It went from a population of about 6,000 to about 55,000. The growth started with a new grocery store, then a new restaurant, then a bank and a car dealership, and then we even began to get new chain restaurants, etc.

It was an amazing thing to see how this little town of Ramona was changing into something new. We felt bad that our little town was growing up, but it was a good thing and even necessary in some ways. Its growth did one more thing: it made our Mobile Home Park a great investment.

It was in September of 1969 that we bought the Park from the Mersmans, who had bought it as an investment from an old Ramona family who started the Park, the Dukes. We owned a piece of property in Las Vegas at the time, and we used it as a down payment, gave the Mersmans an additional $25,000, and paid all the fees, including escrow. The total figure was approximately $230,000.

As I said, the area was developing quickly and by the mid 1980s we began to get unsolicited offers from the local Realtor. The offers became significant enough that my wife and I actually discussed it for the first time. Of course, we had no desire to sell the Park, but we weren't unhappy about how much our Park had appreciated.

Even though we weren't interested in selling, we didn't put a stop to the occasional offers, and I'm not sure we could have even if we'd wanted to. Besides, we knew that prices were rising all over the county and thought we could at least keep track of what the current market value was for our Park.

We were happy with our lives and weren't looking for change. We had friends and acquaintances living in the Park, and we had grown close to and were comfortable around them. We were attached not only to the beautiful area, but to the friends and neighbors we had made there.

About five years after we bought the Park, we bought the property bordering us, and we figured that we'd build a home on it and run the Park from there. But we were in no hurry to do so. We were enjoying our retirement and, despite the responsibilities of running the Park, we had enough time to travel occasionally, as well.

Most importantly, we had our health. Neither of us were on any medication, despite our ages, and we knew that the stress-free life we had made for ourselves was even a better return on our investment than the financial security.

For us the Park had become more than an investment. It had become a great part of who we were as people.

3
Enter the Sessas

Sometime in 1990 while I was doing chores, a man approached me and introduced himself as Paolo Sessa. He claimed to be interested in buying the RMHP, even though he knew it wasn't on the market. I explained to him that I was not interested in selling, and he said he understood.

We talked a bit more and he seemed nice enough. I told him that I ran the Park with my wife, Elizabeth, and that we were quite happy with our life there. He asked if I'd mind if he came by again sometime to show his wife just how beautiful the location was, and I said "Okay."

He told me he was an engineer and that he worked at North Island for the government. He also said that he and his wife were licensed real estate agents and that he had met her in Los Angeles after he moved there from Canada. But he was originally from Sicily, and he seemed proud of that fact.

Paolo brought his wife, Pauline, with him the next time, and it wasn't long before they were coming up to look at the Park nearly every other week. They always visited with Elizabeth and me, always bringing gifts. And what lovely gifts they were: bottles of wine, expensive chocolates, bouquets of flowers, etc. We thought them very nice and extremely thoughtful, if a bit extravagant.

And after just a few visits, they began greeting us with kisses on the cheeks, as close family members do. It was very strange to us at first, but we assumed that it came from their Italian culture. Kissing may mean different things in different cultures, but we have always thought of it as an act implying respect, honor and caring to the one who was kissed. We didn't see any harm in that, and we wanted to be courteous.

As the weeks passed, we found ourselves visiting with Paolo and Pauline as often as we had the time available. Once while they were visiting us Paolo made me promise that if we ever did decide to sell the Park, we would give them the first shot at it. Of course, I agreed. It seemed a harmless promise.

We had become very close to them, and they acted as if they were very close to us, like family. They would take us out to dinner to the nicest restaurants and buy us fabulous meals. They treated us like royalty, buying us expensive wines and champagnes, and still bringing us gifts such as flowers and the like. They treated us very respectfully and, it seemed, sincerely. It was wonderful being treated so well and it was nice not feeling so socially isolated.

We were even invited to join them for very special occasions such as their children's birthday parties, which were held at exclusive restaurants. Their children were very nice. We only met them a few times, but they seemed to be very well behaved and wonderful children.

In fact, at some point, Elizabeth and I had confessed how we had always wanted children, but couldn't have any. It bothered us at times, especially around holidays, but we figured that it just made our love for each other stronger, and we said so.

Soon after that Paolo started telling me how much I was like a father to him. At first, I was a little shocked, but I was flattered as well. I confess I had always desired to hear it, but had accepted that I never would. It was a wonderful feeling, to think of myself as a father figure to someone.

We had, of course, often observed other parents, watching how they were teaching and offering guidance to their children. And we have at times thought about what it would have been like to have children of our own and, I guess, we thought that this was partially what it must be like.

Still, it was quite surprising how Paolo and Pauline were treating us, as if we were their own flesh and blood. Nevertheless, we had no other thought at the time but that they were sincere and genuine.

Then one day during a visit, Paolo shifted the discussion to my health. He began by asking how I was feeling generally, and then his questions became quite specific.

"How's your heart?" he asked. He quickly followed with other similar questions.

Now, the only one who has ever been concerned for me like that was Elizabeth, so it was very strange for me to hear these questions from another person. He also asked how old I was, and at that time I was 74. Then he asked how my memory was.

"Fine," I said. "Why do you ask?"

"Well," he said, with what looked like a concerned smile on his face, "my father is 75 and he can't even remember the names of his own grandchildren."

I wasn't sure exactly what to make of this interest of his, but I guess when you get into your 70s, no discussion of your health seems out of place. Indeed, my health and especially memory became a topic of conversation every time we got together.

I did get a little tired of being asked how my memory was. I began to think that perhaps I was saying something to him that made him suspect that it was going, and I mentioned this to him more than once after he brought it up.

"I was just wondering," he would reply casually.

He seemed sincere and I honestly thought he was truly concerned for my well being. In hindsight, I guess maybe I actually allowed myself to imagine that this was what fathers experienced, this kind of familial concern.

About six months after we first met, Paolo brought his father over to visit. He asked if they could take a look around the RMHP, so I agreed and walked them around. They spoke mostly in Italian, but I understood some of what they were saying. I was raised in a multicultural neighborhood in the East and had heard a lot of spoken Italian.

At one point, and to my great surprise, I heard Paolo Sessa tell his father, "This Park will some day be mine."

As I said, I was quite taken aback by what he had said to his father, but I wasn't necessarily angry with Paolo for making that statement. After all, we did have a casual verbal agreement that if I ever decided to sell the RMHP, he would be the first to know.

He might have been truly anticipating owning the RMHP some day, or maybe he was just trying to impress his father and so he said what he did. However, to hear him talk about how he was soon going to own my property was unsettling. I did feel he was being a bit pushy. My wife's comment at the time was that the Sessas must be really much more interested in buying the place than we had understood.

Paolo and his wife continued wining and dining us quite regularly. They took us to such fancy places as the Coronado Hotel and the like. This type of thing was quite a change for us. We hadn't had much of a social life outside the Park before we met them. We certainly didn't have cause to eat out that often, but they always had occasions for a fancy dinner.

He and his wife continued to visit us at the Park regularly, and things came up in conversation that seemed strange but, in retrospect, may have had a purpose. Of course, at the time I thought he was just making conversation, though I didn't like what he was saying.

For example, I remember one occasion when we were talking outside by the pump house about the Harvey Milk case. It was in the news and on television about how Milk had shot two people, and for this terrible act, he was sentenced to only five years in prison.

At this point in the conversation Paolo looked at me and said, "Oh, isn't this a great country! You can commit murder and what do they do to you? In fact, the bigger the crime, the less time you get in jail."

He noted sarcastically that the murderer had killed two men, and that was why he had gotten only five years in jail.

"If he had killed only one man, his sentence would have probably been only two-and-a-half years," Paolo said. And then he concluded, "Stupid Americans."

It wasn't a very nice way for Paolo to think about our country. I served in the South Pacific, and talk like that didn't sit well with me. But I figured who was I to judge him for what he perceived to be justice, and I said nothing. I probably should have started questioning right then as to whether or not he was the kind of man I'd want to do business with, but I did not.

Paolo also talked often about how we in America pay too much in taxes. Now who wouldn't agree with a statement like that? When asked, I confess I gave him the stock answer.

"If you could," he asked, "wouldn't you like to save money and pay less in taxes?"

"Of course," I said.

He smiled and told me not to worry.

"When it comes time to sell the Park," he said, "I'll talk to you again about it."

And Paolo brought up the Park at every opportunity, and he started to get a little pushier, wanting to know when I was going to be ready to sell it to him. I did discuss it with Elizabeth from time to time, and it became more and more a topic of conversation between us, but we didn't feel ready yet.

As I said, I thought he was a little aggressive by bringing it up so often, especially since I told him that I would let him know when I was ready, but I assumed that he was just an excitable person, anxious to know that I was going to sell it to him and not to someone else. I assured him that we would sell it to him and his wife if and when the time came.

When we thought about it, we realized that Paolo and Pauline had become our very close friends over this two year period. We still had our old friends at the Park, but we would be right next door to them once we got our home built on the adjacent property.

So, eventually, Elizabeth and I began to think seriously about selling the RMHP, and, of course, we could think of no one else we would rather sell the Park to.

Main Entrance to RMHP

4
Blind Trust

Elizabeth and I discussed selling at length, often well into the night. We talked about the little Mobile Park we had purchased almost thirty years ago. We talked about all the friendly people we had come to know over that period of time. We talked of how our little Ramona Valley had grown.

And we talked about our ages. We weren't getting any younger and were now both in our 70s. We even talked about the possibility of living in another city or state, but the only thing that stuck was to develop our adjacent property and live out our lives in the area we loved and close to our friends.

So we finally decided to sell. It was a pivotal moment in our lives, one of those moments where you stand at a fork in the road, make a decision and hope that it's the right one.

The next time Paolo called me, I told him what he wanted to hear, that we were ready to sell.

He came over the very next evening.

He and his wife and Elizabeth and I went into the kitchen and sat down at the table.

He asked me what I wanted for the Park, and I told him that I wanted $1,000,000.

He said no. I was just a little surprised and then asked him what he would be willing to pay for the RMHP. He grabbed a piece of paper and a pencil and explained that he was going to write down a number on the paper. He wrote down $800,000. I refused, and then he spoke up.

"What is the least that you would be willing to take for this Park?" he asked.

I thought for a second and was about to say $950,000, but decided that $900,000 would be enough for my wife and me to live on comfortably, and I told him so. He wrote down $900,000 on the paper and then looked at his wife. She looked pale, but she nodded yes.

Paolo agreed, and so it was settled to sell them the Ramona Mobil Home Park for $900,000.

At that moment I realized that I was selling something that I had worked so hard and long to attain, something that had taken years and years to pay for and many hours invested to maintain. I was not just selling the Mobile Home Park. I was selling the many pieces of myself that I had invested in the Park every time that I replaced a light bulb, cleaned up one of the mobile home lots, or helped someone move in.

But, as I said, Elizabeth and I had decided we could have a modular home placed on the piece of property we had purchased years ago adjacent to the RMHP, be close enough to the friends we had made at the Park, and not have to do all the work necessary to maintain the business.

Paolo and I had made our agreement as to the selling price of the Park. That was the first step—and a big one. We now had to work out all of the details of the sale.

It had been many years since I had bought the Park and I hadn't paid much attention to how the specifics of the sale were being done at that time. Even if I had, things had probably changed so much with real estate that I doubt I would have learned anything truly helpful.

However, I knew that we would still need a place to live for a while and a place to keep our tools, so I insisted that I'd agree to the lower selling price only if he'd allow us to keep our mobile home at the Park and store our tools there until we were ready to move out completely.

He said that he could readily agree to that. In fact, he could use us to manage things at the Park until he got up to speed with the day-to-day workings of owning a mobile home Park.

It seemed reasonable, appropriate even. I trusted in everything Paolo said, and for a long time after, I didn't think twice about following his instructions implicitly. After all, he was the expert, or so he had claimed.

He had claimed that his life and livelihood was in real estate. It was what he did. Paolo seemed to know exactly how and what I should do to sell him the Park. I trusted him very much and allowed him to explain all of his plans.

He said he that he had $100,000 in cash and that he would be selling one of his properties to get the rest of the 20-25% that we wanted for a downpayment. He went on to say how he would be paying us monthly on the principal of $700,000 at 9% interest. He also asked if there would be any penalty if he paid off the principal amount faster, and I said no.

After we had most of the plans ironed out, he came up to me while we were alone and said, "How would you like to save a lot of money on taxes?"

Well, as I already said, who wouldn't? He went on to describe what is called a blind trust and how we could use it to save money. It didn't make very much sense to me, so I suggested that we talk it over with a lawyer before we actually went through with it.

He assured me that it was all completely legal. He explained that the cost of a lawyer was a waste.

"After all," he asked, "we know as much as lawyers, anyway, don't we?"

This gave me pause, but I eventually agreed. I could do nothing else at that time except completely trust him. He suggested to me that I should take his payments on the blind trust and not report them to the IRS.

Paolo explained to me that Americans are stupid in the way that they do everything on credit and with checks. According to him, using cash was untraceable by the IRS, and therefore not taxable.

"Cash is the way to go," he said.

After it was decided not to have an attorney look over this blind trust business, I asked Paolo to explain how it would save either of us money on taxes. Well, it seemed quite complicated, but the way it would end up working is that he would pay me cash, cash that I would not report as income and that, therefore, was not taxable. He explained that it was all legal because it was done with unreported cash transactions.

What he would do is divide the $900,000 sale price of the RMHP into two items. The escrow amount of $500,000 with a blind trust amount of $400,000. The first amount would be paid through escrow, and the other would be paid through the blind trust. In addition, the $400,000 blind trust amount would be interest free for a period of two years and then interest would be charged at 9%.

This was a little confusing to me, but he was very convincing that he understood everything, and he acted as though this was how it was done all the time. He wrote the figures down on a piece of paper to illustrate.

$900,000

100,000 D.P.

1ST @ 9%
400,000

NO INTEREST
400,000

20 YRS
@ $1,500/MO

Believing him to be an honest and trustworthy man, I took him at his word. After all, he had never shown himself to be dishonorable or dishonest to me before. In fact, as I've said, he seemed almost like family by now.

He was to pay us $100,000 of the $500,000 at the closure of escrow and $100,000 of the $400,000 blind trust at the same time. The $200,000 would be enough to develop and build our new home on our adjacent property.

A few days after we agreed to terms, Paolo and I went through the entire Park, through every garage, storage area, etc. I showed him the things that were mine and things that went with the Park so that there would not be any dispute as to what belonged to whom.

One garage contained several boxes of things that had sentimental value to my wife and me, but that were not the RMHP's property. We agreed that I could continue to store the items there until I had my new garage built.

"Everything in this garage is ours," I said.

"Everything in this garage is yours," he repeated.

I then took him to another garage where there were many boxes filled with stuff that I no longer had any use for. I explained to him that everything in that garage was his if he wanted it, or he could just throw it all away.

"This garage goes with the Park," he said.

There was no misunderstanding about what went with the Park and what didn't. We walked back to our wives, and as we approached, I told him very specifically, again, that our personal mobile home was not part of the deal, but that he could have both of the small trailers that Elizabeth and I owned—one that we had for the worker and the other that we had bought from a tenant—and an antique dump truck that was left here by the former owners and that we considered part of the Park.

I showed him the two trailers and the antique truck. I even wrote a note to the DMV stating that these specific items were to be sold with the Ramona Mobile Home Park, and I gave the note to Sessa as proof of the fact. I wanted there to be no possibility of confusion as concerns our mobile home.

I reminded him that I didn't have any place else to store all of my tools and equipment so I would continue to store my things in the garage and rec hall at the Park until I could get them moved to our adjacent property. He agreed again that it would be all right to do so for the six months that we continued to live at the Park.

> To D.M.V. Representative;
>
> I wish to bring to your attention, that I let the foregoing vehicles go with the sale of the Mobile Park.
>
> 1952 Studebaker Truck
> 1976 Shasta Trailer
> 1985 Layton Trailer
>
> Thank you for taking care of this matter.
>
> Yours truly,
> Michael M. Caperich

We also agreed that my wife and I would be allowed to live at the RMHP for six months rent free. I figured that would give us enough time to get all the permits needed and our modular home in place for us to move into. All that I would need was the $200,000 to complete things.

He was agreeable to all the conditions and asked me when would be a good time for me to sign the papers at the escrow office. He said he would be ready the next day if that was all right with us.

I told him it would be and that 10 a.m. would be a good time, and he said that would be fine.

I assumed that we would meet at the escrow office at that time and go over every detail together. I felt I still needed more understanding and would hopefully get it while the specific details of the papers were being composed. I guess I assumed Paolo would take any time necessary to do so.

However, the next morning when Elizabeth and I arrived, we found that he had been there since at least 9 a.m., maybe earlier, and that the paperwork had been completely written up without the hoped for discussion.

I asked to take a look at the escrow papers and agreements, and in a moment I realized I was being severely taken advantage of. There were all sorts of papers, some different versions of the same papers with varying figures. Also, there was nothing that specifically described the "blind trust" or the other $400,000 at all. Though there were many papers that had that figure on them, there was none that clearly spelled out that portion of our agreement.

I was getting a sick feeling in the pit of my stomach.

Looking back on it, I now know that he was juggling the figures and various papers in order to confuse me. Nothing that we had agreed upon verbally was clearly set down on paper.

To my dismay, I found no mention of the payments from the blind trust. In fact, the papers seemed to mention the second $100,000 as if it was part of the "above the table" $500,000 figure, whereas our agreement was that it was to be from the $400,000 blind trust, as he had called it.

Being a little in shock at what I was seeing, I took Paolo aside and asked to see him alone. We walked together outside and I immediately turned to him.

"What the heck are you doing?" I said. "Where is the mention of the money that you promised?"

He acted surprised that I had any questions at all and he explained to me that he would pay every cent that he promised to me when we were sitting at the kitchen table in my house. He seemed angry that I would question him.

He then handed me a check for the first $100,000 in escrow payment. He said that I had nothing to worry about, that I would get a second check for the second $100,000 out of escrow payment. I was still confused about everything, but I took the check.

RAMONA, California, SEPTEMBER, 18TH, 1992

Received from PAOLO AND PAULINE SESSA

herein called Buyer, the sum of ______ Dollars $______

evidenced by ☐ cash, ☐ cashier's check, ☒ personal check or ☐ ______, payable to ESCONDIDO ESCROW

, to be held uncashed until acceptance of this offer as deposit on account of purchase price of FIVEHUNDRENDTHOUSAND DOLLARS NO/100 Dollars $500,000.00

for the purchase of property, situated in RAMONA, County of SAN DIEGO, California, described as follows: RAMONA MOBILE PARK, 2030 BLACK CANYON RD., RAMONA, CA 92065

1. FINANCING: The obtaining of Buyer's financing is a contingency of this agreement.

A. DEPOSIT upon acceptance, to be deposited into TO SELLER OUT OF ESCROW $100,000

B. INCREASED DEPOSIT within ______ days of Seller's acceptance to be deposited into ______ $______

C. BALANCE OF DOWN PAYMENT to be deposited into ESCROW on or before C.O.E. $100,000

D. Buyer to apply, qualify for and obtain a NEW FIRST LOAN in the amount of ...... $______
payable monthly at approximately $______ including interest at origination not to exceed ______%,
☐ fixed rate, ☐ other ______ all due ______ years from date of origination. Loan fee not to exceed ______. Seller agrees to pay a maximum of ______ FHA/VA discount points.
Additional terms ______

E. Buyer ☐ to assume, ☐ to take title subject to an EXISTING FIRST LOAN with an approximate balance of ...... $______
in favor of ______ payable monthly at $______ including interest at ______% ☐ fixed rate, ☐ other ______. Fees not to exceed ______.
Disposition of impound account ______
Additional Terms ______

F. Buyer to execute a NOTE SECURED BY a ☒ first, ☐ second, ☐ third DEED OF TRUST in the amount of $300,000
IN FAVOR OF SELLER payable monthly at $2,500.00 ☒ or more, including interest at ______% all due 20 years from date of origination, ☐ or upon sale or transfer of subject property. A late charge of ______ shall be due on any installment not paid within ______ days of the due date.
☐ Deed of Trust to contain a request for notice of default or sale for the benefit of Seller. Buyer ☐ will ☐ will not execute a request for notice of delinquency. Additional terms ______

G. Buyer ☐ to assume, ☐ to take title subject to an EXISTING SECOND LOAN with an approximate balance of ...... $______
in favor of ______ payable monthly at $______ including interest at ______%
☐ fixed rate, ☐ other ______. Buyer fees not to exceed ______.
Additional terms ______

H. Buyer to apply, qualify for and obtain a NEW SECOND LOAN in the amount of ...... $______
payable monthly at approximately $______ including interest at origination not to exceed ______% ☐ fixed rate, ☐ other ______, all due ______ years from date of origination.
Buyer's loan fee not to exceed ______. Additional Terms ______

I. In the event Buyer assumes or takes title subject to an existing loan, Seller shall provide Buyer with copies of applicable notes and Deeds of Trust. A loan may contain a number of features which affect the loan, such as interest rate changes, monthly payment changes, balloon payments, etc. Buyer shall be allowed ______ calendar days after receipt of such copies to notify Seller in writing of disapproval. FAILURE TO NOTIFY SELLER IN WRITING SHALL CONCLUSIVELY BE CONSIDERED APPROVAL. Buyer's approval shall not be unreasonably withheld. Difference in existing loan balances shall be adjusted in ☐ Cash, ☐ Other ______

J. Buyer agrees to act diligently and in good faith to obtain all applicable financing ______

Court's Ex. 1
Case # 010808
Rec'd ______
Dept ______ Clk ______

K. ADDITIONAL FINANCING TERMS: ______

L. TOTAL PURCHASE PRICE $500,000

We went back inside and he crossed out sections of the paperwork and placed another paper before me that seemed to conform more closely with the escrow half of our agreed upon figures.

But there were many other papers that he threw in front of me that day. One page was a list of yearly operating expenses that we had worked up a few weeks earlier. It seemed to have at least the correct figures for the $500,000 portion of the sale price, but there wasn't in it nor in any of the other papers any explicit mention of the $400,000 portion of our agreement, what Sessa said would be a "blind trust."

RAMONA, CA.

RAMONA MOBILE PARK - 2030 BLACK CANYON ROAD
PRICE $500,000 DOWN 20% $100,000
LOAN $400,000 OWNER WILL CARRY - 20 YRS.

ANNUALIZED OPERATING DATA

YEAR		INCOME	MONTH	
$76,080	$83,040	RENT	$6340	6920
1,200 -	960	STORAGE	100	80
2,460	1680	LAWN	205	140
1,980	3120	ELECTRIC	165	260+
2,868	3900	GAS	239	325+
1,296	960	LAUNDRY COINS	108	80
$85,884 -	$93,660	*WATER REST ROOM	$7157	$7805
			580	
			$773.7 MONTH	

ANNUAL	EXPENSE
50 $1,440	TAXES
00 4,156	INSURANCE
00 1,419*	WATER
00 1,646+7	TRASH
00 278	PHONE
00 218	PERMIT-FEES
00 12,000	PAYROLL
0 2,500	SUPPLIES + REPAIRS
$23,657	

SPACE RENTALS

4 SPC. @ $195 = $780
9 " " 210 = 1890
4 " " 220 = 880
9 " " 230 = 2070
3 " " 240 = 720
$6,340 MO
$76,080 YR
6,960
$83,040 YR
— $93,660 —

Then, while I was reading, Paolo came over to me with another piece of paper. It was an escrow paper and it read that "All oral agreements and contracts are legally binding." At that point I breathed a sigh of relief, believing that I had all the reassurances and protection I needed.

The truth is that any time you are dealing with money, there is always a little bit of nervousness and doubt. So, knowing this to be the case, I just brushed my doubts aside and continued to review the contractual agreements and make sure to ask any additional important questions.

I immediately found problems. For example, in one of the documents it stated that our mobile home in space #18 was included in the sale of the Park. I had specifically told Paolo that our mobile home was NOT included in the sale.

He said, "Well, we will just cross it out then."

He looked for a pen and couldn't find one. Then he picked up a highlighter and marked it in yellow and said that it would be taken out later.

Lots 46, 47, and 48 of VALLE DE LOS AMIGOS, in the County of San Diego, State of California, according to the Map thereof No. 656, filed in the office of the County Recorder of San Diego County, March 6, 1891.

EXCEPT from Lot 46 the Northeast 564 feet.

EXCEPT from Lot 48 the Southwest 460 feet.

NOTE:
At the end of this contract, everything that is part of this contract shall remain the sole property of PAOLO &PAULINE SESSA and/or their heirs, after paid in full.

INVENTORY:
Mobilehome Space N.18,situated at 2030 Black Canyon Road, Ramona,California, in the County of San Diego, together with the following furniture and fixtures, all the equipment that is part of or belongs to the Ramona Mobile Park,Ramona, plus all washers (4) and dryers (3), plus all tools and Shop Equipment, plus everything in the recreation hall, plus one trailer and Studebaker truck and more, including Farmall Harvester and Backhoe and heavy duty trailer.

as security for the payment to Secured Party of Michael Mark Ceperich & Elizabeth Marie Ceperich ($400,000.00) Dollars, according to the terms and conditions of the above Promissory Note, of even date herewith.

Second half of Promissory Note showing the highlighted section. This should have been crossed out in pen, but wasn't.

After a few hours of deliberations, Paolo and I took our pens, signed on the dotted lines, and the title for the Ramona Mobile Home Park moved from my wife and me to the Sessas. A new chapter in our lives was unfolding.

NOTE SECURED BY DEED OF TRUST

(INSTALLMENT-INTEREST INCLUDED-BALANCE DUE DATE)

$ 400,000.00 Escondido , California, October 16 , 1992

In installments as herein stated, for value received, I promise to pay to MICHAEL MARK CEPERICH and ELIZABETH MARIE CEPERICH, Co-Trustees or their named successors of that certain Revocabl Trust Agreement executed February 26, 1987 by MICHAEL MARK CEPERICH and ELIZABETH MARIE CEPERICH for the Benefit of the Ceperich Family or order, at a place specified. the sum of FOUR HUNDRED THOUSAND AND NO/100 ---------------------------------- DOLLARS, with interest from ~~date~~ November 1, 1992 on unpaid principal at the rate of NINE (9.0%) per cent per annum; principal and interest payable in installments of THREE THOUSAND FIVE HUNDRED NINETY EIGHT AND 92/100 ------------- ($3,598.92) Dollars ~~or more~~ on the first day of each consecutive calendar month, beginning on the 1st day of December, 1992

and continuing until the 30th day of October ~~19~~ 2012 , on which day the unpaid balance of said principal sum, with the unpaid interest due thereon, shall become due and payable.

Privilege is reserved to prepay principal in full, or in part, by paying a penalty equal to 6 months additional interest on any principal prepaid in excess of 20% of the original principal balance in any one calendar year.

Each payment shall be credited first on interest then due and the remainder on principal; and interest shall thereupon cease upon the principal so credited. Should default be made in payment of any installment when due the whole sum of principal and interest shall become immediately due at the option of the holder of this note. Principal and interest payable in lawful money of the United States. If action be instituted on this note I promise to pay such sum as the Court may fix as attorney's fees. This note is secured by a DEED OF TRUST to CAL-WEST MORTGAGE CO., a California corporation, as trustee.

Paolo Francesco Sessa Pauline Lydia Sessa

Paolo Francesco Sessa Pauline Lydia Sessa

REV 8/74

DO NOT DESTROY THIS NOTE

This is the document that covered the $500,000 portion of our agreement.

And though I hadn't shared my misgivings with my wife that morning, I could see that she knew something was up.

When all was taken care of, I asked Paolo about the other check. He claimed that he would have to get it together and that it would take him a couple of days. I wasn't happy about that, but what could I do? Indeed, I had a feeling in my stomach that I hadn't felt since I was in the service.

Not only would Sessa's "blind trust," which I never truly understood, turn into a promissory note, which was itself sloppily composed, but his promise to pay me the second $100,000 out of escrow was about to dissolve into smoke.

But more: all the good feeling we had about the Sessas and about selling our Park to people who we had thought as family was also dissolving into smoke. By the time we got home, we were both feeling ill.

PROMISSORY NOTE & SECURITY AGREEMENT 2085

PROMISSORY NOTE
(STRAIGHT NOTE)

$ 400,000 Ramona, California, November I, 1992

after date, for value received, the undersigned maker(s) promise(s) to pay to Michael Mark Ceperich and Elizabeth Marie Ceperich Co-Trustees, or order at Ramona, California the sum of Four Hundred Thousand and no/I00 DOLLARS, with interest from November I, 1992 on the unpaid principal at the rate of [illegible] per cent per annum, payable Monthly $I,500.00 NO INTEREST.

Should interest not be paid when due, it shall thereafter bear like interest as the principal. Should default be made in payment of interest when due, the whole sum of principal and accrued interest shall become immediately due, without notice, at the option of the holder of this note. Interest after maturity will accrue at the rate indicated above. Principal and interest are payable in lawful money of the United States. Each maker will be jointly and severally liable and consents to renewals, replacements and extensions of time for payment hereof before, and at or after maturity, consents to the acceptance of security or substituted security for this note, and waives presentment, demand and protest and the right to assert any statute of limitations. A married person who signs this note agrees that recourse may be had against his/her separate property for any obligation contained herein. If any action be instituted on this note, the undersigned promise(s) to pay such sum as the Court may fix as attorney's fees. This note is secured by a Security Agreement (Personal Property) of even date herewith.

9-30-1992 Paolo Sesso 9-30-1992 Pauline Sessa

SECURITY AGREEMENT
REAL ESTATE & **(PERSONAL PROPERTY)**

THIS SECURITY AGREEMENT is made this First day of November, 1992 by and between Paolo &Pauline Sessa of San Diego, County of San Diego, State of California, (hereinafter "Debtor") and Michael M, & Elizabeth Ceperich of Ramona, County of San Diego, State of California, (hereinafter "Secured Party"). Debtor hereby grants to Secured Party a security interest in all that certain personal property (hereinafter "Security"), now owned or hereafter acquired (except consumer goods acquired more than ten (10) days after the Secured Party gives value, unless those goods are installed in or affixed to such property), and the proceeds and products thereof, described and situated as follows:

First half of Promissory Note showing the interest figures that we'd agreed upon for the $400,000 portion.

5
Small Claims

When Sessa brought me the promissory note, he still didn't have the second $100,000 check for us. A few weeks later, I mentioned it again to him, and he said he was getting the money together. The next time I saw him at the Park, I asked him again for the out-of-escrow payment on the promissory note, and he insisted he would have the money soon. He said he was selling one of his homes, and the deal was almost closed.

In fact, I never saw the second $100,000 that he promised I would receive out of escrow. Over the next few months, I confronted him on the subject numerous times whenever I saw him, which was not so often as it had been. Needless to say, the gifts of chocolates and flowers stopped.

But Elizabeth and I continued to manage the Park for him. And he did pay us both the monthly amount owed on the escrow and the promissory note. However, without the second $100,000 payment, our calculations as to when we'd be able to move onto the adjacent property were completely disrupted.

The weeks turned quickly into months, and since he seemed to be ignoring me on all other channels, I went to his house and asked him what was going on. He explained that he just did not have the money. I asked him why he would even promise to pay it in the beginning if he never had it in the first place. He had no answer to that question.

I tried not to think too much about the other $100,000 payment and concentrated on getting the ground ready on the adjacent property for our modular home. I realized also that I couldn't have the garage built before our agreed upon six month period, so I prepared to purchase a storage container for the items I was currently storing in the garage and rec hall.

I began to realize that as soon as I had laid my pen to paper and signed the agreement with Paolo Sessa, my friend, everything changed. My "friend" became a totally different person. He and Pauline had attained their goal—the Park—and Elizabeth and I were discarded like old hats.

All the visits, gifts, parties, dinners, etc., had stopped immediately after we signed the papers. Whenever he did talk to us, it was only discussions about the RMHP. Everything now was strictly a business relationship and Sessa was all of a sudden very abrupt and cold towards us. I had great difficulty facing the fact that these people weren't what they appeared to be. Elizabeth took it especially hard.

When I realized the effect all of this was having on my wife, I started feeling very bad about selling the Park to Sessa. It didn't turn out like I thought or how I had planned. However, I did sign an agreement and I would honor it with him. I am a man of my word, even though Sessa, at this point, had already broken both the verbal agreement and the written one.

Nevertheless, Elizabeth and I continued to run the Park for him. We collected the rents and handed it all to Sessa every month, all the money. And when he came by to pick it up, he said hardly a word to me, though he still maintained appearances in front of Elizabeth. We also took all the phone calls, met with everybody who had business with the RMHP, and kept the Park in repair.

Since Elizabeth and I still lived at the Park and we had items stored in the garage, I still had a key. Without the second half of the agreed upon initial payment, it was taking longer to complete our new home, so it was useful to have a place to store our tools, etc.

As the months passed, I continued to ask Paolo about the $100,000 out of escrow payment. He continued to give me the runaround.

He said, “Mike, if I had it, I’d give it to you. But I don’t have it.”

This went on for many months, during which time we saw less and less of the Sessas.

Almost a year and a half later in April of 1994, I asked him again for the money, but this time through registered mail. He never responded. I sent him another one in August of that year, but again, he didn’t respond.

2030-18 Black Canyon Rd
Ramona, Cal. 92065
April 4, 1994

Paolo Sessa
4251 Pelon Point
San Diego, Cal. 92130

Dear Paul,
Time is elapsing and I have not had any input from you regarding your promise to pay me $100,000.00 out of escrow. Also, we never received your yearly statement.
Please may I have your response in writing as soon as possible.

Respectfully yours,
Michael Ceprich

Nor did he sign for the letters himself. To my knowledge neither he nor his wife ever signed for them. The notices from the post office always came back with his daughter’s signature. These letters basically asked him why he was having difficulty paying the $100,000 and when he would be able pay it. But, as I said, he never responded.

I told him I needed the money he promised so that we could finish building our new home. He told me that he was trying to sell some property and that he would have the money soon. He asked me to please be patient.

I felt that I had been very patient, seeing as how he promised that I would get the $100,000 as soon as escrow closed. Eventually I said to him once when he came by to pick up the rents that I was going to have to charge him interest at 9% on the promissory note amount. After all, if we were going to have to borrow money, it was going to cost us interest.

Sessa went through the ceiling. He said, "I can't pay that kind of money! Why that would be an additional $40,000! Pauline would have a heart attack."

Sessa cursed at me and even threatened me. I was unsatisfied when he left me that day. I did send additional letters certified but he never responded to me.

2030-18 Black Canyon Rd.
Ramona, Cal. 92065
August 2, 1994

Paolo Sessa
4251 Pilon Point
San Diego, Calif 92130

Dear Paul,
This is another written notice besides many verbal requests for my $100,000.00 you promised to pay me out of escrow.
Please take care of this obligation immediately for I need the money.
A response in writing as soon as possible will be appreciated.
Enclosed is a copy of April 4, 1994 request.

Sincerely,
Michael Ceperich

Then in the fall of 1994, almost exactly two years after we signed the papers, Sessa stopped paying his $1,500 a month on the promissory note. He said that he would not pay any more payments until I put back all the tools and things I took from the garage.

I was taken aback by his accusation. I told him that I didn't have to put anything back because I hadn't taken anything that wasn't mine. Later that day I told Elizabeth and she was incredulous. We were completely puzzled by his behavior at the time, but it wasn't long before his motivations became more than clear to us.

In January of 1995, Paolo Sessa filed suit in small claims court against me. I was served a subpoena to appear in court, so of course I went, although I still could not believe what Paolo was accusing me of.

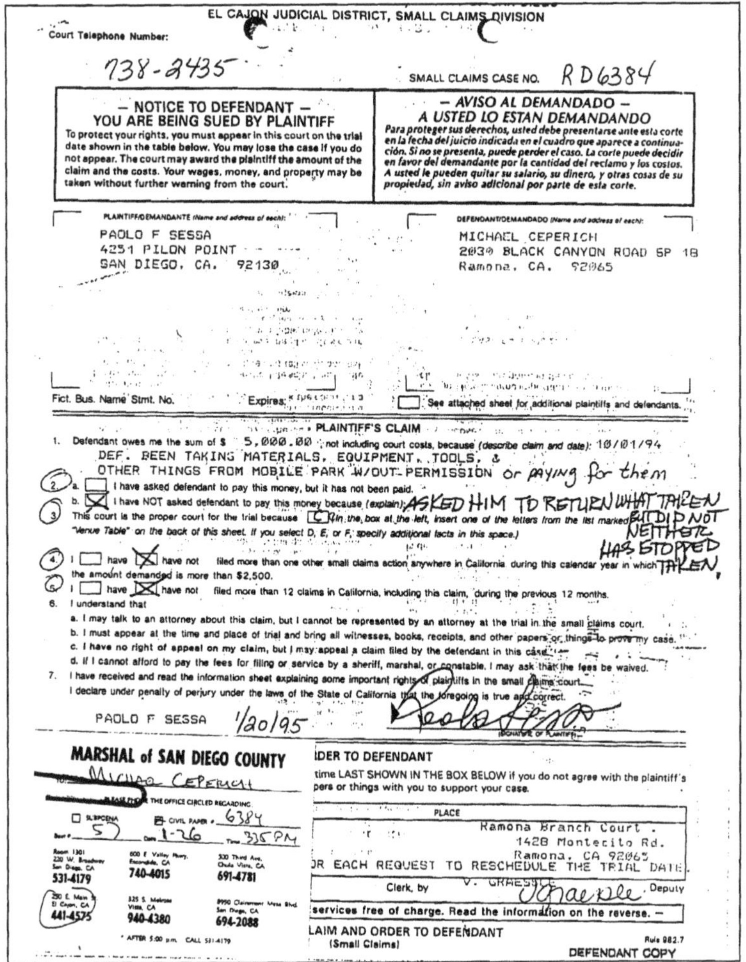

EL CAJON JUDICIAL DISTRICT, SMALL CLAIMS DIVISION

Court Telephone Number: 738-2435

SMALL CLAIMS CASE NO. RD6384

— NOTICE TO DEFENDANT — YOU ARE BEING SUED BY PLAINTIFF	— AVISO AL DEMANDADO — A USTED LO ESTAN DEMANDANDO
To protect your rights, you must appear in this court on the trial date shown in the table below. You may lose the case if you do not appear. The court may award the plaintiff the amount of the claim and the costs. Your wages, money, and property may be taken without further warning from the court.	Para proteger sus derechos, usted debe presentarse ante esta corte en la fecha del juicio indicada en el cuadro que aparece a continuación. Si no se presenta, puede perder el caso. La corte puede decidir en favor del demandante por la cantidad del reclamo y los costos. A usted le pueden quitar su salario, su dinero, y otras cosas de su propiedad, sin aviso adicional por parte de esta corte.

PLAINTIFF/DEMANDANTE (Name and address of each):
PAOLO F SESSA
4251 PILON POINT
SAN DIEGO, CA. 92130

DEFENDANT/DEMANDADO (Name and address of each):
MICHAEL CEPERICH
2030 BLACK CANYON ROAD SP 18
Ramona, CA. 92065

Fict. Bus. Name Stmt. No. Expires:

See attached sheet for additional plaintiffs and defendants.

PLAINTIFF'S CLAIM

1. Defendant owes me the sum of $ 5,000.00, not including court costs, because (describe claim and date): 10/01/94 DEF. BEEN TAKING MATERIALS, EQUIPMENT, TOOLS, & OTHER THINGS FROM MOBILE PARK W/OUT PERMISSION or paying for them
2. a. ☐ I have asked defendant to pay this money, but it has not been paid.
   b. ☒ I have NOT asked defendant to pay this money because (explain): ASKED HIM TO RETURN WHAT TAKEN BUT DID NOT NEITHER HAS STOPPED TAKEN,
3. This court is the proper court for the trial because [C] (in the box at the left, insert one of the letters from the list marked "Venue Table" on the back of this sheet. If you select D, E, or F, specify additional facts in this space.)
4. I ☐ have ☒ have not filed more than one other small claims action anywhere in California during this calendar year in which the amount demanded is more than $2,500.
5. I ☐ have ☒ have not filed more than 12 claims in California, including this claim, during the previous 12 months.
6. I understand that
   a. I may talk to an attorney about this claim, but I cannot be represented by an attorney at the trial in the small claims court.
   b. I must appear at the time and place of trial and bring all witnesses, books, receipts, and other papers or things to prove my case.
   c. I have no right of appeal on my claim, but I may appeal a claim filed by the defendant in this case.
   d. If I cannot afford to pay the fees for filing or service by a sheriff, marshal, or constable, I may ask that the fees be waived.
7. I have received and read the information sheet explaining some important rights of plaintiffs in the small claims court.

I declare under penalty of perjury under the laws of the State of California that the foregoing is true and correct.

PAOLO F SESSA 1/20/95 [signature] (SIGNATURE OF PLAINTIFF)

MARSHAL of SAN DIEGO COUNTY
To: Michael Ceperich
PLEASE PHONE THE OFFICE CIRCLED REGARDING
☐ SUBPOENA ☒ CIVIL PAPER # 6384
Beat # 57 Date 1-26 Time 335 PM

Room 1301, 220 W. Broadway, San Diego, CA 531-4179	600 E Valley Pkwy, Escondido, CA 740-4015	300 Third Ave, Chula Vista, CA 691-4781
250 E. Main St, El Cajon, CA 441-4575	325 S. Melrose, Vista, CA 940-4380	8950 Clairemont Mesa Blvd, San Diego, CA 694-2088

* AFTER 5:00 p.m. CALL 531-4179

[OR]DER TO DEFENDANT
[...] time LAST SHOWN IN THE BOX BELOW if you do not agree with the plaintiff's [...]pers or things with you to support your case.

PLACE
Ramona Branch Court.
1428 Montecito Rd.
Ramona, CA 92065

[FO]R EACH REQUEST TO RESCHEDULE THE TRIAL DATE.

Clerk, by V. GRAESSLE, Deputy

[...] services free of charge. Read the information on the reverse. —

[C]LAIM AND ORDER TO DEFENDANT (Small Claims)
Rule 982.7
DEFENDANT COPY

Paolo Sessa claimed that I had been stealing from the Park and taking things from the garages and he was suing me for

$5,000! Sessa claimed that all of the things in all of the storage areas belonged to him.

When I had suggested that he write down an inventory of the items, he said that we didn't need an inventory. He had always acted as if everything was clearly understood, and at the time I believed him.

I might have guessed that he had heard me say that "everything goes" when we walked into the second garage area, and he assumed that I was still talking about the previous garage. But in retrospect, I realized that he probably never intended to do anything but steal as much as he could from us.

He wasn't concerned that anything be clearly kept in records as he was probably planning from the start to take everything he could. At the time, he would have said anything to pacify me as he was happy enough just to have gotten his foot in the door.

But stealing was something that I had never done and would never do. I sold the place to him and had no interest in any of the things that were no longer mine. The fact that he was accusing me of doing the very thing that he was guilty of was an eye opener.

At that moment I realized that this relationship with Paolo Sessa was not ever going to get better and was only going to continue to get worse. To accuse me of stealing when we had a very clear agreement was unconscionable. And now he wanted me to pay him $5,000 for the use of my own tools!

My attorney, Joe Schiaretta, was willing to help me with the preparation of my defense for small claims court. He helped me organize and document my case, and he had pictures taken so that I could present them in court. Luckily, I had kept copies of papers documenting what exactly was included in the sale of the Park and what was not.

Sessa, on the other hand, produced many handwritten, undated documents that I had never seen before. One especially stood out. It specifically claimed that #18, our mobile home, belonged to him. I knew then and there that Sessa was a liar and completely dishonorable.

It became painfully obvious that his highlighting of the passage in the one previous document instead of crossing it out with pen was no accident. He was already at that point starting to set up a paper trail to obfuscate our agreements and to facilitate his cheating us. The handwritten "so called" agreement to sell him our mobile home reinforced our worse fears.

FOR THE ESCROW OFFICER
INFORMATION:

1- PAOLO & PAULINE SESSA (BUYERS), ARE BOTH REAL ESTATE AGENTS, LICENCED IN THE STATE OF CALIFORNIA.

2- BUYERS WILLING TO GIVE SELLERS 6 MONTHS FREE RENT ON SPACE #18 MOBILE HOME.

3- THE MOBILE HOME ON SPACE #18 NOW PROPERTY OF MR & MRS CEDERICH (SELLERS) WILL BE SOLD TO MR & MRS SESSA (BUYERS) OUT OF ESCROW FOR THE PRICE OF $34,000 INCLUDING FURNITURE PAYABLE @ 1,500 PER MONTH (NO INTEREST) TILL PAID IN FULL, AND 6 MONTHS FREE RENT STARTING WITH CLOSE OF ESCROW.

When it came time to appear in court, it was just like you see on TV, you know, the People's Court. Our judge, Her Honor Margaret Riggs, was very nice and not at all fooled by Sessa's ploys. When Sessa started whining and complaining, trying to sweet talk her, she shut him up. She wouldn't listen to it. She instead asked me to explain the situation about the tools, so I did.

I told her our little agreement about the garage. I told her that I had even kept a key to the garage because my tools and things were stored in there.

I said, "How Sessa could have possibly misunderstood when I told him very clearly that those things in the one garage were my own and that I was not selling them, I don't know."

I told Judge Riggs that Sessa agreed to allow me to store them in the garage until I had my new storage unit built and never asked me for rent.

I also started to tell her about our verbal agreements, but Sessa broke in. He produced a recent letter to us that supposedly spelled out the whole issue.

TO: Mr. & Mrs. Ceperich

This letter is to notify you of the fact that you have not been paying rent on space #18. As of Jan-1 -95 you owe rent as follows:

November first 1994	$385.09
December first 1994	$407.45
January first 1995	$377.04
Total due	$1169.58

More importantly, the mobile home in space #18 has been paid in full as of October 1, 1994, for the agreed price of $34,000. This includes all the furniture. Actually, you have been $500.00 overpaid. You have received 23 payments of $1,500.00 each = $34,500.00. If you wish to continue occupying the mobile home in space #18, you may do so after applying and signing a new rental agreement with the Park as of November 1, 1994 at the agreed rent of $700.00 per month, plus utilities. You also need to start paying for the garage that you have been using free of charge since you sold the Park to us. The rate for the garage will be $30.00 per month starting with November 1, 1994. (KEEPING THE GARAGE FOR YOUR OWN USE WAS NOT PART OF THE DEAL, MUCH LESS WITHOUT PAYING AND WITHOUT PERMISSION).

Mr. & Mrs. Ceperich, you have 10 days from the day you receive this notice to update your illegal status and do the following:

1 - Sign and mail to us the title of the mobile home as being paid in full.

2 - Pay all that is due and restore your rental status, if you decide to stay.

3 - Pay all that is due and vacate; surrender the premises, if you wish to leave the park.

4 - Return all park keys and residents keys to us at once, regardless if you decide to stay or leave the park.

5 - You must stop taking materials and equipment from the park at once or you will be denounced to the proper authorities.

6 - You must stop trespassing on our property at once or you will be reported to the proper authorities.

7 - Turn over the telephone to us and let us conduct our business.

We sincerely hope this is clear and that this matter will be resolved in good faith, gentleman like, or legal action will start within 10 days from the receipt of this notice.

NOTE: As for all the items you took from the park without our permission, we want to inform you that you have been sued in Small Claims Court. Also, we could serve you with a 3 day notice at once, as we have been instructed to do so by our attorney and evict you from the park at once, but we rather give you one more chance.

As you know you have been fully warned twice before, man to man. This is the third and last time.

You also know that the Ramona Mobile Park and everything in it is now our property.

San Diego, January 19, 1995

Respectfully
Ramona Mobile Park

This letter, which we received just days before the court date, claimed that his payments to us that we understood to be for the blind trust/promissory note portion of the sale of RMHP were actually for the sale of our mobile home!

It also stated that our use of one garage was not part of the agreement—again, a lie.

I told Judge Riggs my side of it and about the promissory note.

Then Sessa's real motivation surfaced as he produced the promissory note and tried to get the judge to throw it out, claiming it wasn't valid.

"This document is no good," he said. "It's the same as the other one."

He still hadn't paid me the $100,000 out of escrow payment that we had agreed upon, and now, years later, he was trying to negate the only document that showed he owed me the $400,000 at all.

A chill passed through me. The picture had become frightfully clear to me: Sessa was trying to cheat us out of almost half of the true value of the Park, in essence claiming that we'd sold it to him for only $500,000! I was beginning to feel sick to my stomach.

Judge Riggs asked to see the document, and Sessa handed it to her. She looked at the promissory note for about a minute and then handed it back.

She asked Sessa, "Is this your signature?"

Sessa said, "Yes, but—"

She interrupted him: "This document looks good to me. You signed it."

Relief washed over me. The judge reaffirmed that it was in fact valid and that Sessa had to pay me the $400,000 amount indicated on the promissory note.

The judge also ruled in my favor regarding his suit, so I did not have to pay Sessa for the use of my own tools. I felt as though I had received a little bit of justice that day, but it would be short-lived.

This Security Agreement also secures: (a) any and all extensions or renewals of said promissory note; (b) the repayment of all sums, including but not limited to legal expenses, that may be advanced or incurred by Secured Party for the maintenance, protection or preservation of the Security, or any part thereof; (c) any and all other sums that may hereafter be advanced by Secured Party to or for the benefit of Debtor; (d) any and all other expenditures that may hereafter be made by Secured Party pursuant to the provisions hereof; and (e) any and all other debts and obligations of Debtor to Secured Party that may hereafter be incurred.

Debtor shall execute such Financing Statements and other documents and do such other acts and things as Secured Party may from time to time require to establish and maintain a valid, perfected security interest in the Security; and Debtor shall permit Secured Party and Secured Party's representatives to inspect the Security and/or the records pertaining thereto from time to time at any reasonable time.

Debtor shall keep the Security in good condition and repair, and shall not use it for any unlawful purpose; and shall not remove, nor permit to be removed, any part of the Security from the above premises without the prior written consent of Secured Party, which shall not be unreasonably withheld; and shall provide, maintain and deliver to Secured Party physical damage and loss insurance policies covering the Security in amounts and with insurance companies satisfactory to Secured Party, naming Secured Party as loss payee, as Secured Party's interest may appear.

Debtor hereby declares and warrants to Secured Party that Debtor is the absolute and sole owner, and is in possession of all of the Security, and that the same is free and clear of all liens, encumbrances, adverse claims, and any other security interests. Debtor shall not sell or offer to sell or otherwise transfer the Security or any interest therein without the prior written consent of Secured Party; nor shall Debtor sell, assign or create or permit to exist any lien on or security interest in the Security in favor of anyone other than Secured Party, unless Secured Party consents thereto in writing. Debtor shall, upon Secured Party's request, remove any unauthorized lien or security interest on the Security, and defend any claim affecting the Security; and Debtor shall pay all charges against the Security, including but not limited to taxes, assessments, encumbrances and insurance, and upon Debtor's failure to do so, Secured Party may pay any such charge as it deems necessary and add the amount paid to the indebtedness of Debtor secured hereunder.

If Debtor fails to make payment of any part of the principal or interest as provided in said promissory note at the time and in the manner therein specified, or if any breach be made of any obligation, promise or warranty of Debtor herein contained, then the whole principal sum unpaid on said promissory note, with accrued interest thereon, shall immediately become due and payable, without notice, at the option of Secured Party, and Secured Party, at its option, may: (a) sell, lease or otherwise dispose of the Security at public or private sale; unless the Security is perishable and threatens to decline speedily in value or is a type customarily sold on a recognized market, Secured Party will give Debtor at least five (5) days prior written notice of the time and place of any public sale or of the time after which any private sale or any other intended disposition may be made; (b) retain the Security in satisfaction of the obligations secured hereby, with notice of such retention sent to Debtor as required by law; (c) notify any parties obligated on any of the Security consisting of accounts, instruments, chattel paper, choses in action or the like to make payment to Secured Party and enforce collection of any of the Security herein; (d) require Debtor to assemble and deliver any of the Security to Secured Party at a reasonably convenient place designated by Secured Party; (e) apply all sums received or collected from or on account of the Security, including the proceeds of any sales thereof, to the payment of the costs and expenses incurred in preserving and enforcing the rights of Secured Party, including but not limited to reasonable attorneys' fees, and the indebtedness secured hereby in such order and manner as Secured Party in its sole discretion determines; Secured Party shall account to Debtor for any surplus remaining thereafter, and shall pay such surplus to the party entitled thereto, including any second secured party who has made a proper demand upon Secured Party and has furnished proof to Secured Party as requested in the manner provided by law; in like manner, Debtor agrees to pay to Secured Party without demand any deficiency after any Security has been disposed of and proceeds applied as aforesaid. Secured Party shall have all the rights and remedies of a secured party under the Uniform Commercial Code in any jurisdiction where enforcement is sought. Debtor agrees to pay all costs incurred by Secured Party in enforcing its rights under this Security Agreement, including but not limited to reasonable attorneys' fees. All rights, powers and remedies of Secured Party hereunder shall be cumulative and not alternative. No delay on the part of Secured Party in the exercise of any right or remedy shall constitute a waiver thereof, and no exercise by Secured Party of any right or remedy shall preclude the exercise of any other right or remedy or further exercise of the same remedy.

It is further agreed, subject to applicable law, that upon any sale of the Security according to law, or under the power herein given, that Secured Party may bid at said sale, or purchase the Security, or any part thereof at said sale.

Debtor warrants that if Debtor is a business entity, the execution, delivery and performance of the aforesaid promissory note and this Security Agreement are within its powers and have been duly authorized.

If more than one Debtor executes this Security Agreement, the obligations hereunder are joint and several. All words used herein in the singular shall be deemed to have been used in the plural when the context and construction so require. Any married person who signs this Security Agreement expressly agrees that recourse may be had against his/her separate property for all of his/her obligations to Secured Party.

This Security Agreement shall inure to the benefit of and bind Secured Party, its successors and assigns and each of the undersigned, their respective heirs, executors, administrators and successors in interest. Upon transfer by Secured Party of any part of the obligations secured hereby, Secured Party shall be fully discharged from all liability with respect to the Security transferred therewith.

Whenever possible each provision of this Security Agreement shall be interpreted in such manner as to be effective and valid under applicable law, but, if any provision of this Security Agreement shall be prohibited or invalid under applicable law, such provisions shall be ineffective to the extent of such prohibition or invalidity without invalidating the remainder of such or the remaining provisions of this Security Agreement.

IN WITNESS WHEREOF, Secured Party and Debtor have executed this instrument.

Second page of promissory note

6
2.3 Million!

After the small-claims experience, I refocused in earnest my time and attention on preparing my other property. I now had more motivation than ever to get out of the Mobile Home Park. The past two years, since we had sold the Park to the Sessas, had been a stressful nightmare for Elizabeth and me. But the pressure was affecting my wife more. I knew I had to get the both of us moved out, and the sooner the better.

As for the money that Sessa owed us, I figured that even if he didn't pay us the agreed upon $100,000 out of escrow payment, he was at least legally obligated to pay off the $400,000 note. Her Honor had indicated so in small claims court.

Of course, it wasn't the judgment that Sessa wanted, and it wasn't too long after the small claims court issues were settled that Sessa filed a civil law suit against us for amounts totaling 2.3 million dollars!

I couldn't believe it. There were a number of complaints stated, but the main one was for breach of contract. The irony was overwhelming. He was suing us for the very thing that he was guilty of. If there was any doubt at all of his true nature, it was now gone. We had fallen prey to the worst kind of person.

Sessa was suing us for $50,000 in general damages, $782,670.54 in special damages, and $1,500,000 in punitive damages.

The papers were overwhelming, filled with lies and distortions. What Sessa had tried to do in small claims court—to set up a paper trail of false accounts of our verbal agreements—he was now attempting in California Superior Court.

In these court papers, Sessa claimed our oral agreement was for a $500,000 total selling price for RMHP, that the out-of-escrow promissory note was actually the original written agreement between us for that amount, and that we subsequently amended this agreement and then signed the secured deed-of-trust note in escrow for the same amount, but at different payment and interest rates.

So, again, he was trying to cheat us out of the $400,000 out-of-escrow selling price.

6. Subsequent to executing the afore-described Promissory Note and Security Agreement, on or about October 16, 1992, Plaintiffs and Defendants amended the agreement by renegotiating the payment terms of the purchase agreement. The parties cancelled the Promissory Note, and each party agreed to destroy their copy. The parties then entered into written Escrow Instructions and executed a Note Secured by Deed of Trust, attached hereto as "Exhibit B" and incorporated by reference herein. The amended agreement required monthly payments of $3,598.92 for a term of twenty (20) years, including nine percent (9%) interest on the principle for the purchase of the Park real property and business, as shown in the escrow instructions.

7. On or about November 4, 1992, a dispute arose as to inclusion of the mobilehome situated at Space 18 within the subject purchase agreement. The Plaintiffs did not want to start a legal dispute at that time, so the parties agreed that Plaintiffs would separately purchase the mobilehome at space 18 for the total sum of thirty four thousand dollars ($34,000.00), to be paid at the rate of one thousand five hundred dollars ($1,500.00) each month until paid, and at that time, Defendants would convey to Plaintiffs title to that mobilehome.

Moreover, he again claimed that his payments to us on that promissory note were actually for our mobile home, the one that he had highlighted rather than crossed out on the promissory note, the mobile home that we had agreed was *not* to be included in the selling price.

The agreement was that we were to be allowed to stay rent-free in our space as payment for our help in managing the affairs of the Park and also for our not charging interest on the promissory note.

The preliminary injunction was received by our attorney, Joe Schiaretta, in April of 1995. It was sent by Walters & Ward and it claimed not only that my wife and I had failed to relinquish ownership of the mobile home at space 18, *our* mobile home, but also that we were illegally fencing off property and stealing chattels belonging to the Park.

So at least part of it dealt with issues that I thought had already been settled in court.

Mr. Schiaretta had been our attorney for a long time. He had helped us prepare for small claims court, and he knew most of the pertinent details of our problems with Sessa. So I was very surprised when he asked for an $8,000 retainer to handle our defense, especially since I was stretched a little thin financially, what with the costs of building our new home without the benefit of the money that Sessa owed us.

But I was even more surprised when I asked him if he would give me eight to ten days to get him the money.

"I have to have it now or you will have to get yourself another attorney," he said.

I was shocked at first by the amount that Schiaretta was asking for, as it had suggested the seriousness of our predicament. But why couldn't he wait until the end of the month for his retainer?

I was hurt by this. Sciarretta knew I was good for the money, so I couldn't figure out why he gave me this ultimatum. Looking back on it, I wonder if it was not so much that it was a difficult case, but that it was R. Michael Walters who he'd be up against.

Maybe it was because Walters was such a well-respected attorney that Sciarretta didn't want to get involved, or maybe Sciarretta knew something else, but regardless, it was obvious that he didn't want to take the case. So I was faced with finding a new attorney to help us with this law suit.

It was just two months ago that we'd thought we'd won our point in court. Now things were again extremely disheveled and stressful in our lives. The look on Elizabeth's face was frightening to me. I tried to assure her that Sessa would not get away with this scam, and I immediately set about looking for another attorney.

I asked the real estate broker, the one who had made the early offers to buy the Park, about getting an attorney, and he recommended Kenneth Zalud. Zalud had worked for Walters, the attorney who had done some work for me earlier, but who was now representing Sessa.

We went to see Zalud and he agreed to take our case. In fact, he was excited about taking our case and promised to get after Sessa and expose his fraud. He said that we would counter-sue Sessa, which pleased me.

I gave him a $1000 retainer and agreed to pay him $800 a month as a fee. Not only did he take much less for a retainer, but he acted confident that he knew how to handle this law suit. I felt vulnerable in more than one way, and I was grateful that I had someone on my side against Sessa's onslaught.

As I thought back to Sessa's attitude toward the United States justice system, things were becoming clearer. He actually thought that he could get away with anything.

All Sessa's negative comments about our justice system, comments that I took as just meaningless irrational patter, were now playing back in my head like on a tape recorder.

How could I have been so blind?

The next few months were hectic and painful. According to our new attorney, Sessa was again claiming that he had purchased the RMHP for $500,000, and he was denying the existence of the promissory note. The money that he had been paying us on that promissory note, the $1500 per month, Sessa now claimed was for our mobile home in space #18 at the Park, and that he had paid it every month until it was paid off.

The figure he used was $34,500. He had even supplied a document that he had written, in his own handwriting, that showed the payments of $1500 per month and stated that the mobile home had been paid for.

I never saw this document, but it made no logical sense, regardless. If anyone should have a document that stated paid in full, it would be me, and I had none. When Sessa's attorney showed me the document later at my deposition, I told him that I'd never seen it.

"Well you're seeing it now," he stated sarcastically.

On the escrow papers Sessa had used a highlighter to mark out the part where our mobile home on space #18 was included in the sale. But he never removed it later as he said he was going to do. As you know, when you photocopy any document with yellow highlighting, it generally does not show up, so the sale of the Park, according to his photocopied document, included the sale of the mobile home in space #18.

It really infuriated me that he claimed the $1,500 payments he made since the very beginning were going towards the purchase of the mobile home, not towards the $400,000 promissory note.

I told Zalud that I had been applying his payments to the promissory note, not the purchase of my mobile home. When Sessa sent me the letter stating that he had purchased my mobile home, it was the first I had heard of it. When the promissory note was shown to be binding in Small Claims court, I thought the issue was settled.

I talked to Zalud about these things and he was always sympathetic to our plight and eager to help.

"Mike," he said, "you and Elizabeth are honest people. You can live with yourselves. We all know that Sessa is lying through his teeth."

In retrospect, I might have been too gullible at the time, too eager maybe to expose Sessa for what he was, but it was indeed comforting to know that someone like Zalud was on our side.

I insisted that we have a jury trial, as I felt that a group of my peers would surely see through Sessa's deceptions, and Zalud agreed. He told me it would be a jury trial.

Then came the most important document to date as far as exposing Sessa's lies. In his forensic accounting, Sessa claimed to have made all kinds of improvements to the Park property—specifically, a water heater, louvered doors and a chandelier in the recreation room, among other things.

When I went over to the Park to see these items, I discovered that the water heater was the same one I had bought a few years ago at Home Depot. I still had the receipt for it. And as for the louvered doors and chandelier, well, they were nowhere to be found. I suspected that Sessa paid for them with RMHP money and put them in his own fancy home down in Solana Beach.

Sessa further claimed in his forensic accounting that his worker who lived on the property was making all kinds of repairs, including $520 to clean mobile home #2. I personally went over there and asked the worker, Martin Estrada, if he had been doing all these things that Sessa claimed. Estrada flat out told me that he had not been doing that and he had not been paid to do it, either.

I told Zalud about these and many other of Sessa's claims which were out-and-out lies. He told me to mark them all, every page that had a specific claim that I could prove to be a lie, and to bring in the document in the morning.

Elizabeth and I stayed up late into the night pouring over the ½ inch thick document. We marked every page with a yellow sticky note and highlighted the false claim on the page. It was a grueling but eye-opening experience that left its mark on us both physically and psychologically.

Well, I was even more eager to be heard in front of my peers as I was sure that they would see through Sessa's lies easily. So the next morning when I handed the document to Zalud, I again expressed my eagerness to expose Sessa's lies before a jury, and I was again told by Mr. Zalud that I would have a jury trial. I said that I was looking forward to being heard by a jury of my peers as I knew justice would be served, and he agreed.

Though the shock of initial action brought against us by Sessa had taken its toll on us, things seemed to be going well. And our counter suit against the Sessas was apparently having an effect. Sessa now admitted to the existence of the $400,000 promissory note and even that the selling price had been $900,000 total.

4. Plaintiffs concede that, in spite of both parties' initial confusion over the terms of the agreement, Plaintiffs now hereby ratify that agreement, that, as alleged by Defendants in the related Cross-Complaint at page 2, lines 18-23, on or about September 30, 1992, at Ramona, California, Plaintiffs and Defendants entered into an oral agreement for the sale of the Park to Plaintiffs in exchange for Nine Hundred Thousand Dollars ($900,000.00).

5. The parties agreed to execute two notes and escrow instructions:

A. One unsecured Promissory Note for Four Hundred Thousand Dollars ($400,000.00) at no interest, with payments at One Thousand Five Hundred dollars ($1,500.00) per month until paid, with payments to begin on November 1, 1992;

B. A down-payment of One Hundred Thousand Dollars ($100,000.00) to be paid through escrow; and

C. One Note Secured by Deed of Trust for Four Hundred Thousand Dollars ($400,000.00) at nine percent (9%) interest, payable at Three Thousand Five Hundred Ninety-eight Dollars and Ninety-two cents ($3,598.92) per month for twenty (20) years.

They admitted as much in their Notice of Amount of General & Specific Damages Sought dated 6-26-95. Evidently after his attorney discovered the information that was kept from him, Sessa was forced to admit to our agreement.

In order to legitimize his position, Sessa began again to pay us the $1500 per month amount stated on the promissory note, beginning with a check of $12,000 to make up for the unpaid months.

Banking On America

PAOLO SESSA
PAULINE SESSA
4251 PILON PT. (619) 259-7838
SAN DIEGO, CA 92130

4554
16-66/1220

6-25 1995

Pay to the Order of MICHAEL & ELIZABETH CEPERICH $ 12,000.00

Twelve thousand and no/100 Dollars

Bank of America
La Jolla Plaza Branch 1102
4380 La Jolla Village, Suite 100
San Diego, CA 92122 (619) 452-8400

Valued Customer Since 1978

PAYMENT ON PROMISSORY NOTE OF
For SEPTEMBER 30, 1992

:122000661:4554 110 25 05158

WITH OUT WAIVER OF RIGHTS

I informed Zalud of this and I immediately received a letter from him informing me that Sessa had amended his claim and was no longer suing me for 2.3 million dollars. But along with this good news, Zalud also advised me to hold any payment checks Sessa sent to me and not cash them.

"Why would I want to do that for?" I asked him.

"It will be good evidence," he said.

Then I asked him, "Why wouldn't photo copies of the checks be good enough? Then at least I would get my money."

He insisted that I not cash them and hold them until needed, and he never gave me any further explanation. Appropriate or not, I didn't question him further. After all, it did seem that he was doing some good. And though I wasn't informed as to how the case had changed specifically, it seemed that things were changing for the good.

The checks continued until August, 1996. I had $34,000 in checks placed in an envelope just sitting there. And it was money that we could have used. We were ready to start looking at modular homes and the prices were steep. But we didn't cash those checks.

What now? Well, we had sent letters to our congressman, the district attorney, and the state real estate board, all to no avail. So, needless to say, this was very good news.

July 5, 1995

Michael and Elizabeth Ceperich
PO Box 2109
Ramona Ca 92065

Re: Ceperich adv. Sessa

Dear Mr. and Mrs. Ceperich:

GREAT NEWS!! Enclosed are copies of the Sessa's amended complaint and answer to our cross-complaint. They no longer deny the existence of the $400,000 zero interest unsecured note, are seeking to have the court affirm the original contract (total price $900,000), and are no longer suing you for 2.3 million dollars.

While this is a giant step in the right direction, they continue to deny fraud and fraudulent intent, claiming a big misunderstanding. What a bunch of Bull-@#$%!! Their answer claims a $12,000 payment to get caught up on the unsecured note. Do not cash this check, and in fact if it is in an envelope, do not even open the envelope. See the letter I faxed and mailed to Walters this date.

Call me immediately, even if it is Saturday or Sunday--943-0848. I will be out of the State Monday July 17th (6:00 a.m. to 11:00 p.m.) on personal business, but I will be back Tuesday morning.

Hope you had a wonderful Holiday!

Very truly yours,

Ken

KENNETH J. ZALUD
ATTORNEY AT LAW

We did send another letter to our congressman, Duncan Hunter, asking him to set up an audience with DA Paul Pfingst concerning fraud of seniors. Though things seemed to be turning around generally, Elizabeth and I agreed that informing our congressman about our predicament and asking for more help was not inappropriate.

We were in such a state that anything at all positive seemed like a godsend, and as I said, it seemed that Mr. Zalud was indeed earning his pay. And as peculiar as it seemed to me that we should not cash Sessa's checks, we did as he asked.

Thinking back on it, I wonder if it wasn't Walters himself, Sessa's attorney, who convinced him of the validity of the promissory note. I say this because in late August of 1995, not even two months after filing his suit, Sessa officially changed his attorney to N. Monroe Merrick.

I remembered when Sessa told me he didn't need attorneys. Now it seemed he was going from attorney to attorney. He was probably caught in his lies by his first attorney, Walters, and so he made a change.

And with this change, Sessa was again claiming that he hadn't intended to pay $900,000 for the Park. As I said, I figured that his previous attorney had called him on the issue after he'd seen all the evidence that we had, so now Sessa had to regroup with another attorney.

When we were told about this change of attorney by Zalud, he went on to say that Merrick was "good buddies" with Judge H.R. Hollywood, who was, officially, the scheduling judge for our case.

At this point, Elizabeth and I began our weekly drive down to the courthouse. We drove down there every Friday for the next six months, among our occasional trips to Zalud's office or to take care of some other business concerning this case. It was not a pleasant time for us.

For the rest of that year, we were overcome with papers to sign and interrogatories to answer. They began in late September with forms for personal information and continued on with interrogatories in October and November, each one more intrusive and more troubling for two people our age.

Since, with the change of attorney, Sessa began again to claim that the selling price of the Park was only $500,000, I questioned Zalud about this. He just said that Sessa was getting himself in deeper by lying through his teeth.

Elizabeth responded to the last series of interrogatories and we got them in the mail just five days before Christmas of 1995. They seemed to be going after her more than me, maybe because they felt she was frail enough to attack. This experience was sucking the life out of the woman I loved, and it was the most painful thing I've ever had to go through.

It was a sad Christmas. We made a pact not to buy each other gifts this Christmas since all this was happening. We went to midnight mass at the Santa Ysabel Mission, which was a ritual for us, but in all other aspects, it was a profoundly sad time.

In January we began preparing for Sessa's deposition. Zalud wanted to get a date on the handwritten note of Sessa's and on the document with the crossed out sections. We took them to Manny Gonzales, supposedly a carbon dating tester. We paid Gonzales $2000 by check that day, but the test was inconclusive. Zalud later asked for another $500 to send the document to Washington DC, and to this day, I'm still not sure what the results were.

Elizabeth and I were at Sessa's first deposition in February of 1996, and he outdid himself for deception. He claimed that he visited us irregularly, and that the frequent visits didn't start until after my wife and I agreed to sell the Park. He claimed not to have brought us the gifts, nor to have said that he thought of me as a father, not until after the sale. He also again claimed that he had bought the Park and *all* the items stored there for $500,000. All lies!

When questioned about the handwritten note that showed a selling price of $900,000, he claimed that he wrote it sometime in June, 1995, as he pondered the misunderstanding we were having over the selling price. He made it sound as if he was as surprised as anybody to find that out. I couldn't believe that he could lie so openly and while under oath.

Moreover, he went so far as to accuse me of the very things that he was guilty of. For example, he stated that he had always wanted an attorney to go over the escrow papers and oversee the transaction, and he'd have gotten one except that *I* had insisted that we not use attorneys!

What gall! My wife and I looked at each other incredulously. He went on to claim that the promissory note was actually the first agreement between us and that the deed of trust was the revised agreement.

During the deposition, I tried to interrupt Zalud twice to point out what I thought were important issues, but he wouldn't let me. He didn't seem angry about this at lunch afterwards, but looking back on it, he may have been.

Or, possibly, he had gotten the results back from DC on the handwritten note, and they were inconclusive, as well. I couldn't see how it mattered anyway as I had the handwritten note, and if Sessa had written it two years later as he had claimed, how would I have a copy?

Regardless, something changed with Zalud around that time. I know for my part, I was beginning to question to myself whether we had the right attorney, and Zalud must have noticed my concern because he began to be less friendly.

He told us at lunch after Sessa's deposition that we didn't have to show up on Fridays anymore. We didn't protest as driving into the city, even if only once a week, was becoming a difficult and tiring event. Besides, in all the visits we made to the courthouse, we'd never even seen the judge.

Despite what I thought was a clear and strong case against Sessa, I was beginning to feel we were losing control of things again.

7
Zalud's Mantra

As I've indicated, a few things happened that caused me to be concerned about our attorney. Mr. Zalud had seemed to be energetic and on top of things when we got started, but little by little, the things we had agreed upon were being changed or ignored.

Also, Elizabeth and I were suddenly out of the loop. Not only were we told by Zalud that we no longer had to show up at the courthouse, but also we were no longer kept informed about the specific events of the trial.

For example, we knew nothing of the deposition of our accountant, Clement W. Morin. Nor were we invited to Pauline Sessa's deposition or, later, to Paulo Sessa's second deposition.

In fact, there was a lot going on that we knew nothing about until the case was over and we got most of the documents from Zalud.

I say most, because he kept many of the documents, such as Sessa's lie-filled forensic accounting. Despite the key nature of this document as concerns the fraud that Sessa perpetrated on us and all the time Elizabeth and I put into marking it for Zalud, we never saw the document again.

Whenever we saw Zalud, I would ask for specific information about the case, but he never gave me any. He would, however, always say things like "We're going to get him!"

But the biggest thing that happened that shows how our predicament had gone from bad to worse was when Zalud told us we were not going to have a jury trial.

Sometime in April or early May of 1996, on a Monday, Zalud came over to our home. We didn't know he was coming, which was not the routine, but we invited him in.

"I have news for you," he said. "They're going to start picking the jury."

"Great," I said. "It'll help us. We can bring out the facts."

Though we were excited about the news, he was nonchalant, as if he had other business to take care of.

We talked briefly about getting the papers together, and he said again that they were going to start picking the jury, that day even.

"That's good," I said again.

Three days later, Thursday, he again came without notice. He said he was in the area. This time he didn't come in and sit down.

"The judge decided to hear the case," he said while standing in the doorway.

"How come?" I was dumbfounded.

"To save you money," was all he said.

He was again nonchalant and he repeated that he was just in the area so he decided to stop in. He left hurriedly.

Nothing more epitomizes the unpleasant roller coaster ride we were on. In the course of four days we had gone from picking a jury to not having a jury trial at all.

We were crushed. The one thing I had always been sure of, the one thing—the American justice system—that I knew I could fall back on, was beginning to fail us. Or was it Zalud?

My understanding was that Judge Hollywood was a preliminary judge. If so, then the case not going to jury trial might be because Hollywood, possibly with Merrick's influence and Zalud's approval, decided to settle it himself.

So then, Zalud's statement to me that the judge decided to hear the case himself without a jury, in order "to save money," was the point at which we lost our jury trial. If this is the case, then Zalud fell short of his responsibility to us by not telling us what was going on. If I had been told that another judge might be hearing the case, I'd have wanted that to occur, and I'd have told Zalud as much.

But I say this now, because at the time, under the weight of all that was happening, all I could feel was betrayal. It seemed to us at the time that we were fighting not only Sessa, but the justice system as well. We were about as distressed over our situation as two people could be. It's only in retrospect that I question Zalud's role in all this.

Yes, I wasn't happy about the wasted money for analyzing documents, but that could have been an honest foul up on Zalud's part. And I figured that his telling us we didn't have to come to court any more was just a part of the way things were done. After all, we had gone to court weekly for nearly six months straight and had never even seen the judge. Everything went on behind closed doors, between attorneys and Judge Hollywood, though I now wonder if Sessa was present, as well.

Any time I asked Zalud about how things were going, he would only say things to me like "We're going to get him" or "You're going to get your Park back" or some other such thing that seemed to imply that everything was going well.

But this losing of our jury trial was the final straw. We felt, once again, alone against the world. The stress was getting to us both, but Elizabeth was especially affected. I had to sort things out

I wondered first why Zalud came to us in person twice that week instead of notifying us by mail or fax or even by phone. I realize now—since I've gone through all the papers provided us after the case, all the papers save the ones that Zalud, to this day, has not given me—that we have no record of these two visits. Could it be that Zalud did not want anything written portraying these visits?

And how could not having a jury trial help *us* save money? I suppose it might have saved the court, and maybe even Zalud, some money, but not us.

The fact that the trial had been changed from a jury trial was my biggest concern, as I was sure a group of our peers would see clearly how my wife and I had been taken advantage of by Sessa. I was sure we would get our Park back and be otherwise compensated for our loss due to Sessa's fraudulent behavior.

As I said, I was also disappointed that Zalud had charged me approximately $2000 to have the first handwritten note checked to see when it was written and that he later told me that he'd need another $500 to send it off to Washington. It confused me at the time as to why he hadn't sent it there in the first place and saved $1500.

Soon after Zalud took the case, he had told us that the Sessas were no longer claiming that we'd sold him the Park for $500,000 instead of $900,000. This changed, and at his deposition, Sessa again claimed that the promissory note for the second $400,000 was part of the original agreement which we later amended, and that the $1500 per month payment was for our mobile home in #18!

Apparently Sessa claimed that he had written the note with the $900,000 figure to himself recently, supposedly after he had realized the misunderstanding in 1995. Zalud was going to prove that Sessa had written the note in 1992 by sending it off to Washington. My question was this: Why did we have to prove when it was written at all? Was Sessa going to claim that I had stolen the handwritten note from him?

I was sure a jury would have seen through this. But it was not to be.

And Zalud continued to say that things were going well and that Sessa was going to get his. A hearing date was set for late May of 1996.

We started to think about going to court again, and I began to insist that we at least be heard by the judge. I didn't want it to be like it was before, when we would just show up with our various documents and sit for hours in an empty courtroom while they met behind closed doors.

We went twice that summer, and on one of those occasions, it was just like it had been before. We sat while they conferred behind closed doors. Then Zalud walked out and told me that the judge had asked to see the checks that Sessa sent me. He commented that the judge was sucking Sessa in and that Judge Hollywood was going to crucify Sessa.

I handed the envelope full of uncashed checks over to Zalud and he took it in to the judge. Zalud came out without the checks.

The judge took them that day and I never saw them again: $34,000 gone. When I later asked Zalud where my checks were, he only told me that the judge had kept them.

"When am I going to get them back?" I asked.

"I don't know," he replied simply, nonchalantly.

Zalud later said that maybe I should have cashed them. But he told us not to worry, that we were going to get Sessa, and that we were going to get our Park back.

As it turned out, we didn't get to show Sessa's fraud, we didn't get the money he owed us, and it took a $160,000 bank loan and months more of grief before we got our Park back.

Not to mention the tens of thousands of dollars it was costing us in court and attorney's fees, or the $34,000 that I'd just given away, or the tens of thousands of dollars we could have made had we just invested the second downpayment that Sessa owed us and let the interest accrue over the years, or even the thousands of dollars it would eventually cost us to bring the Park back to its original condition.

We had sold the Park in good faith and at a fair market value. We had agreed to let Paolo Sessa pay us a large portion of the selling price interest free for a period of time. We had continued to help the Sessas manage the Park, even after they defaulted on the second $100,000 downpayment. In short, we had done everything to be fair and accommodating to the people who had befriended us.

But Paolo Sessa defrauded my wife and me of more than our Park and an incredible amount of money. He took away our happy retirement, disrupting our lives and causing great physical and emotional pain.

What was fair compensation for that?

And when I asked Zalud if these things were being discussed with Judge Hollywood, he would quickly say not to worry, that the judge knew everything, and that Sessa was going to get his.

But I wasn't so sure of that anymore, and I continued to insist that I be heard by the judge. Zalud assured me that I would still have my day in court, even if it were only with a judge instead of before a jury.

The preliminary hearing was moved to August of 1996. It lasted no more than five minutes and amounted to the two attorneys, ours and Sessa's, entering their trial briefs. The judge said something about a settlement, and that was it. Judge Hollywood never said a word to either us or the Sessas.

Afterwards I asked Zalud again about being heard, and he again assured me that the judge would hear me. I told Zalud I would hold him to that.

And eventually we did get heard, if you could call it that.

8
Our Day in Court

On the day after Labor Day, 1996, we drove down for our day in court. I was prepared to tell the judge of our experience with the Sessas and how we had been defrauded by them. I had a folder full of documents with me proving the fact.

Zalud met us outside the courtroom. He told us that it wouldn't be a long proceeding and instructed us to just answer yes to the Judge's questions.

"But what about all the evidence?" I asked.

Zalud said that this wasn't the time for that.

"Don't get the judge upset," he said. "Just answer yes."

I was a little confused, but there was no time to ask Zalud any questions. He led us into the courtroom and we waited for the judge.

Judge Hollywood entered and asked the attorneys to state their appearances for the record.

"Munro Merrick for the plaintiffs."

"Kenneth Zalud representing Mr. and Mrs. Ceperich. And Mr. and Mrs. Ceperich are both present in court."

He turned to us and we both answered yes.

Then the judge asked if the Sessas were present in court, and their attorney, Merrick, answered yes.

"I am the independent calendar judge," Judge Hollywood began. "This case has been under my supervision from the day it was filed—or, they were filed—up until last Friday, when I sent the case over to Judge Meloche, as I was trying to get cleaned up to go on vacation. Judge Meloche asked me to hear the settlement conference, because he felt uncomfortable in a nonjury case to do that. So he asked if I would do that. So I said, 'Of course.' The ultimate result is that it is being transferred back to me for all further purposes. And we've reached a basic settlement approach to it with some things that the court will continue to handle. We'll have a further hearing on the matter, then. And I take it that transfer back to me meets with everyone's approval."

"That's correct," said Merrick.

"No objection, Your Honor," said Zalud.

My mind was racing. I hadn't agreed to the case going back to Judge Hollywood. After being told by Zalud that Judge Hollywood and Merrick were "good buddies," I was eager to have any other judge. But, as I've said, I wasn't in the loop. Nor was I aware that we had reached a settlement with the Sessas.

"All right," Judge Hollywood continued. "you folks know, since I've talked to—to the Ceperichs. I didn't get a chance to talk to the Sessas. It wasn't, obviously, necessary, with your fine representation. It wasn't necessary here. But I did want to talk to the Ceperichs about the situation they found themselves in. I think we've reached a model for our settlement. And we're going to proceed on a minimal basis now to conclude the matter. And council for the plaintiff will please recite the terms of the settlement."

Elizabeth and I looked at each other incredulously. When had we talked to Judge Hollywood? When had we agreed to a settlement? I started to protest to Zalud, but he shushed me, and Sessa's attorney proceeded to give the terms of the settlement.

"Thank you, Your Honor," Merrick began. "Yes. The parties have agreed to a recision of the transaction which was the subject of the lawsuit, that is, the purchase of the Ramona

Mobile Park. Everybody is to get back what they tendered, all consideration on both sides."

Merrick went on to give the specifics of the recision transaction, including the fact that a court appointed forensic accountant would mostly determine the transaction amounts, with Judge Hollywood deciding the remaining issues.

Merrick also said that "the agreement was that we would pay the forensic accountants on a 50/50 basis."

Again, Elizabeth and I had never agreed to anything. We hadn't even known there was an agreement. And if this forensic accounting was anything like Sessa's previous accounting, then all the things that were issues in the past, things that spoke to Sessa's lying and fraud, were far from settled.

When Merrick finished, he turned to Zalud and said, "Counsel, is that complete?"

"No prevailing party," Zalud added. "Each party bears their own costs."

"Yes," said Judge Hollywood. "We talked about that in the settlement conference this morning. That would have been the court's ruling in any event in this case. That's part of the agreement, that you'll bear your own costs and attorneys' fees. And I will want to monitor this fairly through, because these will be court-appointed forensic CPAs."

He went on to say that "the ultimate security for the payment due would be, obviously, the court imposition of a court-established lien on the property so to insure the payment to the plaintiffs of any final, agreed-upon value."

The words "agreed-upon value" rang in my head. If we got the same amount of input in the negotiations for an "agreed-upon value" as we'd got in all the other agreements made to date, Elizabeth and I were completely lost. Indeed, there had been another closed-door conference this very morning, and we had known nothing about it.

The judge then asked if there was any objection to the firm that the court would ask to do the accounting.

"Do you folks have any person that you would want me to consider?"

"Your Honor," Zalud said. "As far as the defendants go and cross-complainants, that would be fine, and we would accept the recommendation."

Merrick agreed, and then added, "There are two other items which I forgot about. Number one, there are some checks which were payments of $1500 a month or so. There's a check for $12,000. Total of some 30-odd-thousand dollars of uncashed checks which the Ceperichs have. Those will be turned back tomorrow morning to the Sessas."

So there it was. The $34,000 in uncashed checks that the Sessas had paid us was gone, money that had been paid us on a legally binding agreement. But it didn't end there.

"Thirdly—or lastly," Merrick continued, "with regard to payment, I think it is the anticipation of everyone that the Ceperichs will be able to obtain an immediate loan on the property of more than enough to cover any potential recision payment."

I couldn't believe what I was hearing. It sounded as if Sessa would not only be getting away with fraud, but he'd also be paid for his trouble!

Judge Hollywood interrupted to confirm that the Park property currently had no encumbrances.

"That's correct," Merrick answered.

But Sessa couldn't restrain his excitement at this point and he said aloud, almost in unison with Merrick's answer, "Yes!"

I'd heard that kind of excitement in his voice before. It sent a chill down my spine, and it must have done the same to Elizabeth because she stiffened and squeezed my hand.

But Judge Hollywood seemed not to notice Sessa. He again directed his question to Merrick.

"So the property is free and clear at this time? Is that what they're saying?"

Merrick answered: "Our assumption at the present time is that, once a figure is arrived at after Your Honor's decision, that there will be basically an immediate payment or as shortly as it can be made after they can make arrangements for the loan. So it might be 30 or 60 days."

I couldn't believe it! It sounded as if it was already settled that we'd have to pay the Sessas to get our Park back!

And it seemed that Zalud had already agreed that we would.

"We anticipate no more than 90 days for the funds after the court's final ruling on the determination," Zalud said. Then he added, almost as if for our benefit, "If in fact the determination is in fact that moneys are owed."

"That's fine," said Judge Hollywood. "I think that's the fairest thing for the parties. It is—by far and away, it will be less expensive. And I will instruct the special masters not to go to any unnecessary work on this matter. If they run into a snag, check with me before they incur any unusual expenses on it. The court will monitor it independently and will need to look at books and records. Not so much the Ceperichs' but the Sessas'. You have the books and records that will be there, utilized by the CPAs, to justify what additional amounts that you want."

The whole time he seemed to be talking to Merrick, and when he asked whether anything more had to be added to the settlement, only Merrick answered: "No."

"All right," said Judge Hollywood. "Would you inquire of your clients, please, of the acceptance of these?"

Merrick turned to the Sessas.

"Both Mr. and Mrs. Sessa, have you heard the terms of the agreement which I've just recited?"

Paolo Sessa answered first and quickly: "Yes."

"Yes," said Pauline Sessa.

Elizabeth squeezed my hand again, as if asking for strength.

"Do you understand them?" Merrick asked.

The Sessas both answered "Yes."

Merrick then asked if they agreed to be bound by them, and the Sessas again both said "Yes."

Merrick then turned back to Judge Hollywood.

"Both parties agree," he said.

Then Zalud turned to us.

"Mr. and Mrs. Ceperich, have you heard the terms of the settlement as recited into record by Judge Hollywood, myself and Mr. Merrick?"

Elizabeth was shaking. It was all she could do to answer, "Yes." I wanted to ask questions, to find out exactly what the hell was going on with all this, but all I could manage was a meek, "Yes."

"And did you understand those terms?" Zalud asked.

Elizabeth couldn't answer, probably because it would have been a lie to say that she understood.

"Most of it, yes," I spoke up, remembering Zalud's instructions to answer "yes" to any questions, but still wanting some explanation. And I was about to ask—I'm not even sure what, exactly, as there were so many questions going through my mind at the time—but Zalud quickly interrupted me.

"And do you agree to be bound by the terms and conditions?"

But I was still thinking about my many questions, and maybe because I felt that this might be my only chance to point out at least one of Sessa's lies, I focused in on the ownership of mobile homes.

"As of now, on the mobile home, is that—"

"In terms of that," Zalud interrupted, "do you want to go off the record?" He was looking at Judge Hollywood.

I was lost. I wanted to go on record with my story, but Zalud had interrupted me and was now asking the court for direction.

"Work it out with him," Judge Hollywood said curtly.

"Mr. Ceperich has a question regarding the Mobile home that's presently occupied by Mark Estrada, the worker. And

Mr. Merrick read it into the record that we were gong to have the forensic accountant make a recommendation as to whether that's a legitimate business expense and, thus, property of the Park subject to a recision or expenditure of Mr. Sessa, and, thus, he's entitled to possession of that as his personal property, and then Judge Hollywood would make a ruling on that following the forensic accountant's recommendation."

I'm not sure I had wanted only to focus on that mobile home with my question, but I am sure that Zalud seemed to be acting in a hostile way toward me.

"As long as it is his possession, fine," I began, but that's all I could get in. Zalud wanted to keep me from asking anything else, and he knew that I would.

"Do you understand that term and condition?" he asked.

"I hope you understand me," was all that I could manage in response before he went on.

"And do you understand all the other terms and conditions recited on the record?"

Elizabeth was visibly shaking now. I'm sure she sensed how frustrated and upset I was. I felt beaten down, but I was even more worried for her.

"Yes," I said.

"And do you agree to be bound by it?" Zalud asked.

"Yes."

"Very well," said Judge Hollywood. "This is sort of a settled case. We have a contingency yet to go. And I've already indicated the court's feelings on that. If it's all right with you, I'll go ahead and make immediate arrangements. I know from the past that it won't be a matter of days. It will be weeks for them to come back to me. So the moment I get that report back, I will send copies to both counsel and arrange for a hearing on that matter at that time. So all I need from you folks is just your cooperation with a court-appointed CPA. And they will get the information back. You will have ample time to review the final report before you appear in court. So in case you have any problems with it, I think this is the easiest and fairest way to do it. Otherwise, we'll spend another five or six weeks trying to get somebody to agree to it."

It seemed the court had everything it wanted in place. I was too torn between concern for Elizabeth and frustration at being ignored by my attorney and the court to care whether or not Judge Hollywood got the CPA he wanted or not. But he went on to explain further, nonetheless.

"The court does have some subtle influence on these folks, because they don't normally like to do this kind of work. But because they appear in front of me in court, they are anxious to please judges. Believe me, they are not in favor of one side or the other. They will do a fair job down the middle and report back to the court their findings. And I'll share the findings."

What did he mean by "subtle influence"? And by "pleasing judges"?

"Very well. Thanks very much for your cooperation. I have mixed feelings about this. I thought that I had closed the books myself personally on this. But I'm more than happy to see this now through to the conclusion. I really appreciate the attitude of both parties in this matter. This thing can't work without the parties' cooperation, the Ceperichs and the Sessas. The attorneys are the facilitators in all this, but the ultimate agreement has to be by the parties."

He was sounding like the whole thing was over, and I still hadn't been heard!

"You folks were at one time close friends, and I think this has the possibility of working out to everybody's not necessarily satisfaction, but I think a fair resolution to the parties that are before me. So I thank the parties very much, and I appreciate talking to the Ceperichs this morning."

And with that, he recessed the court.

But there it was again! Why was he saying that he had talked to us this morning when he hadn't?

To be honest, I felt at the time as if I was fighting on so many fronts at once that it was possible we met one other time with Judge Hollywood. But "met" isn't really the right word; it was more like we were in the same courtroom together, along with the Sessas. I believe it was very early on, maybe the first time Elizabeth and I went to the courthouse almost a year ago.

But we never, either Elizabeth or myself, ever got to "talk with" Judge Hollywood or tell our side of the story.

And it could be that we drove down early on that morning and met at the so-called "settlement conference." Maybe it was then that I remember being sworn in, along with the Sessas. As I said, I was in such a state that it was possible. Luckily I had a transcription of this settlement hearing, so I could be precise with it.

But I say it again: neither my wife nor I ever got to talk with Judge Hollywood. We were never heard.

I brought this up with Zalud afterwards, but he just put me off, again.

"I haven't been heard," I said to Zalud. "Is that it?"

"Yes, that's it," Zalud said. Then he added in his usual mantra, "You got your Park back."

"For a price!" I said. "Why do I have to pay to get it back?"

He didn't answer.

It was a horrible drive home. Elizabeth and I talked about what had happened, and we just couldn't believe it. We had known nothing about this being a settlement hearing. We had thought it was going to be the beginning of our trial, not only as defendants, but also as cross complainants.

We had a case against the Sessas! We were suing them as well, and we were expecting to show how we had been taken advantage of by them.

Instead, we had been railroaded by the court, not heard by it. And to judge by Paolo Sessa's reaction, he had gotten exactly what he wanted. What he didn't want was to hear me tell the court how he defrauded us, and I didn't get a chance to.

His attorney got for him exactly what he wanted. Mine had turned a mantra of "We're going to get your Park back" into an excuse for not really representing us at all.

And how could Judge Hollywood say that he talked to us when he hadn't? And the whole thing about the other judge not wanting to hear the case because it wasn't a jury trial?

But that's what I wanted all along—a jury trial!

I felt sick to my stomach on that drive home. And Elizabeth wasn't much better off. In fact, the experience had been harder on her than me. She looked worn and tired in the seat next to me.

Elizabeth had always been the voice of reason, telling me that things were going to work out, that we had truth on our side and that truth still went a long way in this world.

But now she looked tired and beaten. And I felt pretty much the same way.

Just like with Zalud's literal justification for his misrepresenting us, we had had our day in court. But it had only lasted about fifteen minutes, much less time than it had taken us in small claims court.

And we still hadn't been heard, not by Judge Hollywood.

9
Insult to Injury

Though it was said by Sessa's attorney at the hearing that we were to take possession of the Park the very next day, that didn't happen. Sessa's attorney had also said that the Sessas were to remove all their possessions from the Park the next day, but that didn't happen either, not until much later.

In fact, nothing much was different that next day as far as the Park goes. Sessa continued to collect the rents and profit from owning the Park. How this amount was accounted for in the final figure that we paid, I'm still not sure.

To be honest, we were in a daze for the next few months trying to understand what was going on. We no longer went to the city to court or to meet with our attorney, and Zalud was getting harder to get hold of. He wasn't returning our calls as he had in the past.

When I finally did talk to him, he told me that the judge was still on vacation and it would take a little time to conclude things.

"How can we conclude things if I haven't been heard?" I asked him.

"Well, you're getting the Park back," was all that Zalud said.

"Yea, but at what cost?" I said again to him.

Eventually we were told that Judge Hollywood was going to hear us. It was sometime in late October or early November of 1996 when we were supposed to appear, though I am not positive as to the exact date as there is no court record of the meeting.

Elizabeth and I drove down to the courthouse where we were met by Zalud. He said little to us and ushered us into an empty courtroom. There was no court reporter or any other court official present, only my wife and I and Zalud.

Then Zalud left the room, and through that same door entered Judge Hollywood. Present were the judge, my wife and I, and no one else. It was strange.

Judge Hollywood stated that we were both still sworn in, and he proceeded.

"Have you ever been in court before, outside small claims court?" he asked.

"Yes, Your Honor, I was," I said.

"Tell me about it," he said.

I proceeded, telling him that I was in Federal Court when I was eighteen years old for evasion of income taxes. It was an honest mistake made in my youth and the judge excused the $17 that I owed and told me to pay my taxes from now on and to continue to send money home to my parents.

I wasn't sure what this had to do with our case against the Sessas, unless Judge Hollywood was concerned about how Sessa and I did part of the deal for the Park under-the-table.

"Your Honor," I began. I was going to tell him how it was Sessa's idea to do so, and that Elizabeth and I had since paid the back-taxes on the income shown on the promissory note. We had done so two years ago, before our small claims court appearance.

But I never got to say any of this. Judge Hollywood wouldn't let me go on.

"I don't want to hear any 'he said/she said' today," he said.

"No, Your Honor," I said. "I have facts." I was prepared to tell him how we'd been taken advantage of by the Sessas, of how Paolo Sessa had lied to and defrauded us, of how he had lied to the court in his deposition—I was prepared to make my plea for justice before the court.

But it was not to be.

After I said I had facts, Judge Hollywood lowered his head and murmured something, and then he stood up and left the chambers.

Elizabeth and I were now alone in the courtroom. She had never uttered a word. The whole thing took less than five minutes, and we never saw Judge Hollywood again.

We waited and waited for him to reappear, about twenty to twenty-five minutes,

But he didn't show. Instead, it was Zalud who next appeared. He came back into the room through the same door.

"Are you ready to go?" he said.

"Go?" I said. "I haven't been heard. Is that it?"

"That's it."

I looked at Elizabeth and she looked pale. I must have looked about the same. I looked at Zalud, desperately searching for the right words to express how I felt, but unable to think of any.

"Could you give us a ride to Coronado?" was all I could manage.

"Why?" Zalud asked.

"So we can jump."

"You don't want to do that."

"Why not?" I was aggravated. My wife looked like she was about to cry.

Zalud said nothing, but just escorted us out of the empty courtroom. When he left us, Elizabeth was broken hearted and in tears.

"I can't believe it," she sobbed. I kept my arm around her as we walked to the car.

"Everything will be all right," I said to her softly. "We still have each other."

The drive home was even worse than the last one after the settlement hearing. It was clear now that Zalud never intended for us to be heard. He was merely placating us.

Or maybe he was helping Judge Hollywood. Was this meeting simply to cover the judge, to back up what the judge had said on the record at the settlement hearing? That he had talked to us, when in fact he hadn't?

And why wasn't there even a court reporter there? Whatever hope for justice we might have had left after the settlement hearing was now up in smoke. It seemed we were alone against a corrupt world.

While we were driving home that day in a state of despair, my wife first said the words, "Corrupt judge, Corrupt Trial." And they have rung in my head ever since.

That holiday season was even less cheerful than the last. Elizabeth was very ill, and it wasn't long before we had replaced our weekly visits to the courthouse with weekly visits to the doctor.

In the meantime, though we didn't know about it until we went over the court papers much later, the report from the court-appointed accountant came in. It called for us to refund the Sessas their $100,000 down payment plus $21,777 for the value of the various trailers, mobile homes, propane inventory and capital improvements.

Sessa obviously made false statements to the accountant. There was only one trailer, since Sessa sold one of them in the interim, and one mobile home. And if both of these items were truly capital improvements, they were only worth a total of $8000. And Sessa got $1500 for the trailer he sold, which would knock the figure down to $6500.

As for the propane inventory, I had to eventually pay off the outstanding bill on the propane. So I was being charged for propane that I had to eventually pay for anyway. Not to mention that it cost me my good relationship with the propane dealer.

Not to mention also that, by agreement, Sessa wasn't to sell any of the property of the Park, and he did. He sold the antique truck, the trailer that the Park worker lived in, the gas motor for the shredder, and various other items that belonged to the Park.

Also, he didn't sell the backhoe, but he ruined it by using it improperly to remove deep-rooted brush. The worker, Martin Estrada, told me how it happened and how the backhoe began to make knocking noises, but how Sessa told him to ignore the noises and to continue.

When it eventually stopped working, he had Estrada take the motor apart, and there it remained all in pieces, still to this day. I was eventually told that it would cost over $6,000 to repair it.

Nevertheless, despite all these things, Judge Hollywood decided that Sessa should get more money rather than less, supposedly as compensation for his management of the Park, but it was more like mismanagement. Besides, we weren't compensated for the first two years that we managed the Park for Sessa.

The figure that Judge Hollywood arrived at amounted to about $282,000! Instead of compensating us, the victims—for our trouble, for all the money we had already lost due to Sessa's frivolous lawsuit and to his breach of promise—we were going to have to pay him even more money!

When Zalud gave me this figure, I utterly refused.

"Just give him the Park," I told Zalud.

A few days later Zalud called and said that he'd talked them down to $200,000 and strongly advised me to take it. I still refused.

"Just give him the Park!" I said.

Mr. Zalud came back a third time and said that they were not going to make a lower offer than $160,000 and that I'd better take it or they would make me pay the $282,000 amount.

As I said, Elizabeth's health was getting worse. I did feel I could still fight this somehow, but I'd have to wait until I could regroup. So, grudgingly, I agreed to buy back the Park for $160,000.

Sessa would walk away a lot better off than when he came in. The judge dissolved the contract between Sessa and me, and I had to pay Sessa back for all he had invested. But my losses were still accruing.

Elizabeth was heartbroken.

"Why did we ever meet these people?" she said dejectedly and often.

In one of Merrick's papers, included in the stack of documents I received later, he concluded: "the goal of recision is to restore both parties to their former position as far as possible."

Well, this recision didn't return me to my former position as far as possible. I wanted at least a strait recision, since it was Sessa who was breaking the contract. I don't believe I should have paid Sessa anything. And even with a straight recision, I'd have still lost on the deal, especially since the profit claimed by Sessa—$17,400—was considerably lower than what I would have made owning the Park.

Indeed, we had averaged about $100,000 per year as income from the Park when we owned it. Multiply that by the four years that Sessa owned the Park, and it equals $400,000. Of the $9000/month that Sessa pulled in, he paid me approximately $5000/month, which leaves nearly $200,000 in profit that Sessa disposed of somehow, but that I would have had use of as profit had I owned the Park.

At some point after I agreed to the $160,000 figure, Zalud said to me, "Oh, we got him!" and when I asked what he was talking about, he told me that Sessa admitted that he'd made $174,000 in profit owning the Park. This admission by Sessa happened *after* I was forced to agree to pay $160,000 to get back the Park.

I wasn't sure what good this was to know at this point in the proceedings. It should have been brought up earlier, before Judge Hollywood made his stipulation and I had to agree to pay Sessa for the Park, even though it was Sessa who had defaulted on our agreement, not me.

Zalud's mantras of "We got him!" and "Got your Park back!" rang hollow in the end. Zalud was only placating us with his words, again.

But more important, Elizabeth's health was failing quickly. This whole ordeal had taken its toll on us in ways that can't be compensated for. How can one get back one's health?

Judge Hollywood produced his Stipulation for Judgment in March of 1997. Among other things, it stated that we were not to talk to anyone at the Park, which made no sense to me. How could we conduct business while not talking to anyone?

But even more importantly, the stipulation gave us only 60 days to pay the $160,000. We figured to pay off Sessa from the rental money from the Park, possibly $5000 per month until it was paid off, but Zalud told us that we couldn't do that. He said we'd have to pay it all at one time.

So we immediately began to look for a loan. Our local bank manager told us they couldn't make that kind of loan, but he directed us to another that did, and we filled out and submitted the papers.

While we waited for the loan to go through, we got a thirty-day eviction notice and a cynical letter from Sessa. The letter was a notice raising the rent for our mobile home, which was still parked in space #18, to $5000 per month!

Since the final judgment had already been made and the Park was about to be turned over to us again, this was a vicious ploy on Sessa's part to bring my wife and me even more pain than he had already inflicted.

Sessa was being vindictive and trying to agitate us further, as the case was already settled. He was obviously uncaring at best about ruining our health, two retired people in our late 70s, people who he had once kissed on the cheek and called his own.

May 13, 1997

Elizabeth Marie Ceperich
Michael Mark Ceperich
2020 Orange Avenue
Ramona CA 92065

Dear Mr. and Mrs. Ceperich:

You are hereby notified that the rent on the premises currently occupied by you at the Ramona Mobilehome Park, 2030 BlackCanyon Road in Ramona, will be increased to $5000.00 per month effective June 16, 1997. The rental payment in that amount will be due and payable on or before June 16, 1997.

If you fail to pay the rent on or before that date, legal proceedings will be commenced immediately against you for possession of the premises, and damages for unlawfully detaining the property will be $166.67 per day.

Very truly yours,

Paolo Sessa

But he had us by the throat this time, and he wasn't about to relax his grip. He must have figured he'd got what he wanted by changing to a strong-arm attorney, and he was going to keep that pressure up to the bitter end.

In the final papers we found from Merrick, his attorney, an Abstract of Judgment that named Walters and Ward, Sessa's previous attorney, along with us in the Information on Additional Debtors. It seems that the Sessas were involved in an action against Walters, probably for not being ruthless enough.

But more: Since Sessa was about to return the Park to us officially, the eviction notice seemed to have little to do with anything except to harass two elderly people, my wife and me. To the end, Sessa—the same man who used to kiss me on the cheek—was vindictive and hurtful. Even after a judgment that his attorney claimed was in his favor, Sessa struck out at my wife and me. All we had wanted was to be rid of him in our lives, but his ill will was much more far-reaching.

Of course, I'd continued to protest to Zalud and anyone else who would listen that we shouldn't have to pay Sessa at all. If anything, he should have to pay us. But my protests fell on deaf ears. Zalud's litany was, as always, "Well, you got the Park back."

And Zalud was about to augment Sessa's spitefulness with his own final, cynical act.

When the time came for the transfer of the Park, Sessa was to take his personal belongings off the premises. The court had stipulated that he take only personal belongings and nothing that belonged to the Park. Zalud called and said that we were to meet at 2 p.m. the next day to oversee the transfer.

Before we left home that next day, maybe because I remembered how the Sessas had years before shown up early at the escrow office, I told Elizabeth jokingly that they'd probably be already packed with everything from the office.

"They wouldn't dare," Elizabeth said.

But they did.

When we arrived at the office a little before 2 p.m., there they all were: the Sessas, the attorneys, and two cars with trunks and back seats packed full with not only *all* the Park papers, but with other Park items, as well.

I walked over to where Zalud and Sessa's attorney were standing and chatting pleasantly.

"What is going on?" I said to Zalud. "Aren't you going to take pictures of this? They're taking everything!"

Zalud just stood there smiling indifferently.

"Well, Mike," he said, "if you think they have something that belongs to the Park, then by all means look at what they have and take it out."

I was infuriated. I shouldn't have had to look through all the stuff they had jammed into those two cars. They should have had to wait for me and had me authorize what they were to take. Judge Hollywood's stipulation for judgment wasn't being upheld. He specifically stated, "What belongs to the Park was to stay in the Park."

But Sessa was taking everything!

I walked back and looked in one of the trunks and saw a light bulb. Now how could that light bulb not belong to the Park? Disheartened, I picked it up and Elizabeth and I walked into the office.

It looked as if the place had been robbed.

"Michael, you were right. I can't believe it!"

I walked over to the desk, careful not to touch a thing. I wasn't sure why I did that. Maybe it was because I felt as if I was at a crime scene. Drawers had been left wide open and emptied. Even the walls were bare.

I sat down, feeling defeated and violated. Then I reached over and screwed the light bulb, the one and only thing that I had retrieved from Sessa's trunk, into the desk lamp and turned it on. I leaned back in the chair and sighed in disbelief. Elizabeth put her hand on my shoulder, and we waited there in silence.

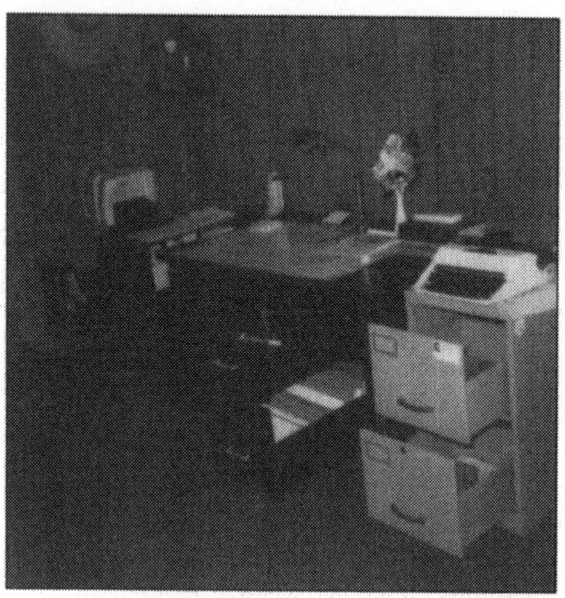

I looked at the emptied office and all that I could see was the picture I had in my mind of the two attorneys standing there in the Park driveway and chatting pleasantly. I tried to think about what I wanted say to Zalud, but I was too numb to think. And so was Elizabeth.

So we just waited there in silence for what seemed like an eternity. Finally, Zalud popped his head through the office door and asked us if we were ready to go.

"I was ready a long time ago," I answered dryly.

We were given the keys to the office, we locked it, and we walked home in silence. I was in despair. I felt that I'd been taken for a sucker by everybody.

I thought, This is what I fought dictators for. On the high seas, from the US Pacific shores to Tokyo, Japan. My three brothers, plus all my comrades, living and dead, we fought dictators on land and sea.

I remembered that I'd lost thirty pounds to illness, but never complained. I'd doctored with the military and on my own. And when I was dismissed from the service the day before Christmas, I stood in front of my wife and she didn't know me.

Finally, I said, "Hi honey." And she smiled and said "Hi sweetie! I didn't recognize you!" And then she asked me what happened, and I told her I'd tell her all about it when we got home.

And eventually, after we got home, that pain subsided.

But the pain I felt on the day Sessa ransacked the Park office only intensified after we got home. I kept replaying in my mind all that had occurred, and I felt sick to my stomach.

I could still see my attorney standing out in the driveway with Sessa's attorney, just shooting the breeze. He was just blabbing. He should have been taking pictures, looking through the documents that the Sessas were taking, looking out for our interest.

I was paying Zalud $250 an hour—and for what?

And what was he talking to Sessa's attorney about?

Frankly I began to believe they were colluding against me. I began to think it was all planned in order to take every shred of evidence so that I couldn't find anything about what Sessa really did with the money or the Park.

Elizabeth was feeling weak and she had to lie down. I decided to walk back to the office to take pictures of the crime scene. Not so much as a paper clip was left. Sessa had taken everything, and the only thing I'd saved was the light bulb out of the desk lamp.

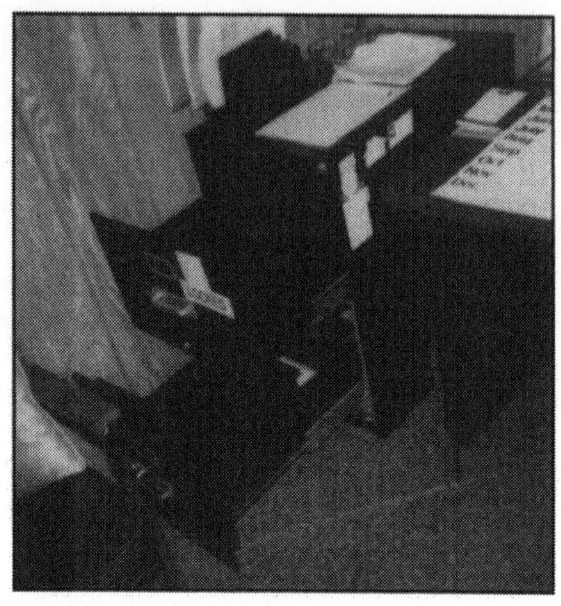

Off the Sessas had gone with every record of the Ramona Mobile Home Park. I didn't have even one lease, one electric bill, insurance policy—*nothing*!

Sessa had taken not only all the current papers for the Park, but also all of ours from the time we owned the Park and all those we had kept of the Mersmans, who owned it before us, and of the Dukes, who owned it before them.

All these papers were taken by Sessa—illegally, as the judge had stipulated that all documents of the Park should stay with the Park.

Sessa also took the current leases which showed who had paid what and how much, deposits and closing rents, etc. We eventually had to ask Zalud to get back the long-term leases for the tenants. Zalud first told us that Sessa claimed he didn't have them, but then, a few weeks later, Zalud told us that he had got them back and we had them again.

But these were the only papers we got back. All the others, including renters' applications and other signed legal documents, the historical records of the Park, we never saw again.

After this meeting, even Elizabeth was disappointed with Zalud, and she showed it. She broke down and cried. I told her to wait in the car and I walked back to Zalud's office.

In his office I confronted him. I told him to his face that I thought that he was colluding with Mr. Sessa's attorney in the driveway at the Park.

"I was not colluding!" he said harshly.

"You were too colluding," I said. "Why didn't you watch what Sessa was doing and take some pictures?"

"Why didn't you say something?" he said.

"You're the attorney!" I said. "You're the one who is getting paid to do this stuff!"

"I'm not going to represent you any more," Zalud said angrily. "You need to find yourself another attorney."

Then he lifted his fist towards my face and made an obscene gesture.

"Fine," I said, and I walked out.

Person, in any manner, or talk to anyone coming on the property for purposes authorized by this stipulation except to identify the visitor as an Authorized Person.

Each party affirms that s/he has reviewed the terms of this stipulation, that s/he understands each and every term and condition, that s/he has consulted with his/her attorney of choice and has discussed this stipulation with said attorney, that s/he agrees to each and every term and condition, agrees to do nothing to impede or hinder the performance of this agreement, and promises to take whatever actions are necessary to assure the faithful performance of all his/her obligations under this agreement.

Should any action or proceeding be necessary to enforce the provisions of this settlement agreement, the prevailing party shall be entitled to recovery of all his/her costs including reasonable attorneys' fees.

/

/

/

/

ORDER

It is so ordered.

Date: March 11, 1997

HARRISON·HOLLYWOOD

Harrison R. Hollywood
Judge of the Superior Court

Last Page of Judge Hollywood's Stipulation

10
Dissolution

So that was it, as far as Zalud was concerned. I will forever remember him as shaking his fist in my face. Evidently he had learned from Sessa and his attorney how to handle elderly people.

As for us, we still had to get the loan for $160,000, and the 60 days that Judge Hollywood had allowed us was not enough. Before the loan came in, a lien was placed on the Park. It was another time of great embarrassment to us, and Elizabeth took it especially hard.

All the tenants were notified to send the rent money to the marshal's office. We were not even allowed to have money for the water payments, which we had to pay regardless. And we never got an accounting for the money which was sent.

But on a personal level, that was the least of my problems. About the time of Judge Hollywood's final stipulation, Elizabeth was diagnosed with both cancer and heart problems. The stress of our lives the past five years had finally caught up with her. She was now seriously ill.

Then, on the day the marshals came to the Park to talk to the tenants, Elizabeth broke down and cried. Again.

I was furious with our situation and what had happened to us. Was there no end to the indignity we were to suffer?

But where could we turn now for help? Everything that we had together just five years previously had been turned upside down. Judge Hollywood's statement that both parties should be returned to their previous state echoed in my head.

How could Elizabeth and I be returned to our previous state? How could one get back one's health?

In June of 1997 we retained Robert W. Zickert as our attorney. It cost us another $5000 to do so, but he handled the legal paperwork involving the lien that Sessa had put on us. He also handled the payment for our half of the court-appointed accountant fees, which amounted to almost $2400.

Even though Zalud was claiming to have won our case for us, I told Zickert about not being represented properly by Zalud, and he agreed that it seemed that it was so. But he advised against pursuing a claim of a mistrial or to appeal the judgment.

Zickert did admit to me that he thought we had been misrepresented by Zalud and that he could have helped us better if he had had the case from the start.

So we started to plead our case in other places.

We sent letters to the *San Diego Union Tribune*, another one to DA Pfingst, and even one to Judge Hollywood. It stated something to the extent that Sessa had more power than the judge. I was referring mostly to the incident at the Park when the Sessas absconded with all the important Park papers, both current and from the past, and my attorney at the time didn't seem interested to help at all with it.

Judge Hollywood never responded to our letter, but we did hear from him otherwise. Through Zickert, our new attorney, we received an Order to Show Cause why we hadn't yet paid the Sessas or the court-ordered accounting fees and to appear in court before Judge Hollywood.

The pressure was on for us to pay the Sessas, evidently because others, including his previous attorneys, had an interest in getting paid through Sessa's settlement with us. In fact, I eventually discovered that Sessa and Walters, his first attorney, had filed actions against each other, Walters for nonpayment of attorney's fees and Sessa for misrepresentation.

And Sessa had a new attorney to pay, though Joseph J. Strazzeri was formerly with Merrick's firm and had assisted Merrick with Sessa's lawsuit.

In any case, it was Strazzeri who contacted the tenants by letter to inform them of the lien and instruct them as to where to send their monthly rents. We were still working on the loan, but I guess it wasn't happening fast enough for all concerned.

Our new attorney handled most of this, and he also got us a copy of Judge Hollywood's Stipulation for Entry of Judgment, which we still hadn't got from Zalud. Zickert also sent a letter to Strazzeri explaining that a loan with Great Western Bank was looking good. However, that loan didn't go through.

Despite her emotional and even physical pain, Elizabeth continued to help with the correspondence. Her illness had intensified her embarrassment and grief over the lien, especially when the marshals came. They had acted as if they were under specific orders not to talk to us or to be at all civil to us.

It was a horrible experience, and it ended, once again, with Elizabeth in tears. After that, she stayed away from the Park entirely as she couldn't face the tenants, so I handled that part.

And it was a mess. All the tenants had been notified to send the rent money to the marshal's office. I wasn't even allowed to have money for the water payments. In fact, the money collected for the next few months was never accounted for. I never saw exactly what they took in and where it went.

But I still had to pay for the water out of my own pocket.

And I still had to get a loan for $160,000.

At the end of the month, one of the tenants approached me and said that, since she was moving out after the next month, and since she had given Sessa the last month's rent, she shouldn't have to send in the next month's rent.

She asked me for the money and I told her that I didn't have any of the money that Sessa had collected. She then called Strazzeri and argued her case. I'm not sure how it all turned out, but later Strazzeri sent me a letter and a bill charging me $17.50 for his time talking to the tenant!

I didn't respond, and I assume he eventually took it out of the lien money he was collecting from the tenants. Just one more person feeding off of the situation. It seemed that nobody would be excluded from benefiting.

Much later, another tenant asked me for her last month's rent, and I asked around. I discovered that Sessa had done this with everybody at the Park. Before, I thought it was just something he did with that one tenant, but Sessa had done it with all the new tenants. Of course, how could I know. Sessa had taken all the Park papers with him.

In August, we got a letter from Zickert stating that our loan from Grossmont Bank had been approved and enclosing a copy of Strazzeri's preliminary accounting from March through July of 1997.

It showed the $160,000 judgment with added fees and interest and subtracted payments from the tenants. I had no idea how accurate this accounting was, as Zalud and the court had never shared with me any of the figures, but it did show what they were currently taking from the tenants.

And at least Zickert was getting information to us, something that Zalud hadn't done. He sent us a copy of his letter to Strazzeri stating that Grossmont Bank was to process a check to Sessas and Strazzeri in the amount of $154,465.31, and he enclosed a proposed grant deed, an Acknowledgment of Satisfaction of Judgment, and a copy of a letter to the tenants informing them of the change.

Zickert also sent us a five-page Release & Settlement Agreement between Walters & Ward and the Sessas. Evidently Walters & Ward were the defendants, sued for professional negligence, breach of fiduciary duty, and breach of contract.

I shivered when I read it. Sessa was pulling the same thing with Walters, so his law firm had not come away from his relationship with Sessa unscathed. But Sessa did pay them $15,000 in attorney's fees as part of the settlement.

In the middle of August our loan went through, and in September the Park was again officially in our names. Of course, we were both quite disillusioned by this time. Elizabeth had given up trying to make any sense of it at all.

Zickert also told us that Strazzeri's argument as far as the condition of the backhoe was concerned was that its condition was taken into account by the $160,000 settlement figure. I argued that I didn't feel it was, but Zickert said that it wouldn't be in our best interest to pursue a separate lawsuit over it.

Nevertheless, Elizabeth sent a letter to Zickert about taxes due on trailers and the many missing things I was finding: a kerosene heater, typewriter, chain saw, cutoff saw, and shredder, not to mention the condition of the backhoe. We took the time to document and list these things, but it seemed the effort was too little, too late.

And our other efforts were equally fruitless and bitterly ironic. In September of 1997 we got two responses to the many letters we sent out to various people.

One was from the district attorney's office, congratulating us for getting a favorable settlement against Sessa. So they finally responded to our letters, after the fact, but it was only to *congratulate* us! For what?

As I've said, I didn't consider the settlement at all in our favor. In fact, it was ludicrous that both our attorney and Sessa's attorney were claiming victory. I could surely see how Sessa's attorney could claim that, but it was quite a stretch for Zalud to do so.

But as Zalud's chorus went, "You got your Park back!" And I guess in his self-serving mind, that constituted a victory. Yes, we got the Park back, but at what cost?

The other letter was from the San Diego Bar and it was in response to our complaint against Zalud. Even though Zickert had advised us against suing Zalud, we decided to pursue some sort of action against him, even if was just to complain to the Bar.

But the letter stated that our complaint was "beyond the scope of [their] activities" and it suggested that we contact the State Bar of California.

Elizabeth was not surprised at this response, as she had suggested when we sent the letter that we'd just be bucking the system. But she kept her chin up and said she would compose a letter to the State Bar.

She sent it off in early October, and by the end of the month, we had their response stating that "errors in judgment and mere negligence, by an attorney, do not form the basis for disciplinary action by the State Bar."

It was the same old runaround. Elizabeth and I consoled each other as best we could. Needless to say, it was still painful to us both. We looked everywhere for possibilities to somehow get the justice we'd been denied. The only thing left was to write a book and share, publicly and in print, our tragic experiences with the Sessas and with the justice system. It seemed the only thing left to do, the only avenue still open to us, and we now began to cling to it for hope.

That Christmas, we broke the ice and gave each other gifts again. It was the last Christmas we would have together.

Over the next few months, Elizabeth's health continued to deteriorate, and she was now in much pain. Finally, in the summer of 1998, Elizabeth passed away. She died brokenhearted and disappointed. She had lost the will to live.

11
Zalud's Revenge

I can't possibly convey just how heartbroken and alone I now felt. For the next few months I forgot about Sessa, Zalud and Judge Hollywood and dealt only with this tragedy.

First were the funeral arrangements. Since I was a veteran, I thought it would be an honor to be buried at the Riverside National Cemetery, and before she passed away, Elizabeth had agreed.

Also, there were many letters to write to relatives, and legal matters to be taken care of, and I did those things as well as I could. It was quite taxing. Seldom did a day go by that I didn't cry.

Slowly I began again to handle the affairs of the Park, and eventually the pain of what they did to us returned. The last years of our life together had been taken away from us by unscrupulous people. They could never know the despair that they caused me, but, despite what they did, I wouldn't wish it upon them.

Then in October of 1998 I got a bill from Zalud for $22,868. It wasn't the first one he'd sent to us, but it was the first time I'd contacted him concerning his bill.

Of course, I wasn't at all happy about paying Zalud anything else, as I didn't feel he'd represented us properly. But when he offered to settle for $15,000, I offered him $10,000 despite my misgivings about paying him anything more at all.

He refused. This whole conversation took place over the phone and it was very short. I believe I mentioned my dissatisfaction at his representation, but there was little else said.

I spent the next few months putting what papers I had received from Zalud in order and preparing to write this book. I was more determined than ever that I would get the truth out about this whole affair.

In April of 1999 I received an arbitration notice. It had my name as the applicant and Zalud as the respondent. It was peculiar as I didn't really apply for arbitration. It was more like I was pushed into it by Zalud. He must have known he would get what he wanted through arbitration.

What I wanted were the papers that Zalud still had concerning the case. I would need them for the book I was writing, and I was willing to pay the $800 arbitration fee just to get those papers back alone.

By the end of the month, I'd received a letter from Lewis, D'Amato, Brisbois & Bisgaard, who was to conduct the arbitration for the Bar. It asked me if I wanted to add any documents or materials to the arbitration panel.

Enclosed were three documents submitted by Zalud: 1) a transcript of the settlement hearing on September 3, 1996, at which Elizabeth and I were present; 2) a report by Roberta Spoon for the court appointed forensic accountants to Judge Hollywood dated December 9, 1996; and 3) a Stipulation for Entry of Judgment and Order filed March 11, 1997.

There were three arbitrators, Zalud and myself present. I told them that I was not properly represented during the litigation. I told them that I wanted a jury trial and that Zalud had promised me that at first, but that changed. Then I had insisted that I be heard by the judge in order to tell my side of the story, but that didn't happen either. I also told them that I was upset that I had to pay an additional amount to the Sessas to get the Park back.

I didn't dispute the amount that Zalud wanted for his work, but I insisted that he give me the papers that he still had that he didn't give me when the case was over: Sessa's original lie-filled accounting of expenses and Elizabeth's and my depositions. There were other papers that he had, but these three were the most important to me now.

Zalud stated that he'd give me the papers if and when he found them, and that was it. To this day I've never gotten those documents.

Zalud also stated that the ultimate goal was to get the Park back and that was achieved. I thought about saying that I also wanted compensation for the money that Sessa should have paid me, but I never got a chance.

The whole thing lasted not much more than fifteen minutes, and to tell the truth, I couldn't get out of there fast enough. It felt again to me as if I'd walked into a situation in which the matter had already been settled before I got there.

In June of 1999, I received a letter from the San Diego County Bar enclosing the Arbitration Findings and Award, among other documents, including a five-page letter from Brodshatzer, Wallace, Spoon & Yip, accountants, to Judge Hollywood recommending the Sessas be repaid their $100,000 down payment "plus $21,777 for the value of the various trailers, mobile homes, propane inventory and capital improvements."

Of course, I should have contested these figures; I should have done so when Zalud came to us with the $160,000 figure, and I would have if I'd had a breakdown of the figures at that point. But, instead, we just had Zalud throwing settlement figures at us. It seems obvious to me now that he only wanted us to settle, at any figure, regardless of fairness.

The documents also stated how Zalud testified that the litigation was contentious and he did a lot of work and consulted experts, etc., but Zalud never said any of this at the arbitration hearing, so when did he testify to all this? As I said, at the hearing it had been like at all the other so-called court appearances: It seemed as if things had already been settled ahead of time.

The document went on to say how Zalud testified that on the morning of the trial, Judge Hollywood initiated a settlement conference, which took place over several days and resulted in a settlement including recision of the purchase and sale agreement. There were additional hearings and arguments before the court regarding the report of the court-appointed accountants.

So when did the arbitrators hear all this testimony by Zalud? I guess they heard all this in the same room that Judge Hollywood heard my testimony. And that was the clincher. The Arbitration Findings ended with these words: "His claims of inadequate representation and an inability to present his side of the dispute to the judge is belied by the minutes of the hearing in open Court wherein the settlement was recited on the record and Mr. and Mrs. Ceperich stated their agreement with it."

So there it was. That's why Judge Hollywood kept saying that he'd talked to us about the case even though he hadn't. Zalud's statement to me at the time that Judge Hollywood and Merrick, Sessa's attorney, were "good buddies" came back to me. I again felt that the whole system had been against me.

In November of 1999 I received an order to Confirm Arbitration Award and for Entry of Judgment Thereon.

But I was not present at this arbitration hearing. I called two weeks ahead of time to change the arbitration date and was told that I should call back a few days before, which I did. At that time I was told by the clerk, a man named Steve, that it was too late to change the date. I had again been taken advantage of.

In early December of 1999, I called the State Bar and talked to someone who was very sympathetic. She told me that it sounded as if we been taken advantage of as seniors and that I should write an official letter explaining my situation.

It was hard to get the sense of all that had happened to Elizabeth and me, but if I was going to write the book, I was going to have to sort through the events and make my case.

So I wrote the letter in December of 1999 and sent it off to the office of the State Bar of California. In it I stated some of the things I had not been able to state in open court or at the arbitration hearing. But it didn't help, except to give me practice at organizing and writing this all down. A week or two later they sent me a letter stating that they were short-handed and couldn't do anything at the present time.

In January of 2000, I sent a letter to the AARP for help finding an attorney. They sent me two names. The first attorney agreed to get the court documents that I had been trying to get from Zalud since the case ended, but he was unsuccessful.

The second attorney I only talked to on the phone. I told him that I was misrepresented by Zalud and that I didn't want to pay him any more money, especially since he still hadn't returned to me the documents that I'd asked for and that I had a right to.

He was not very sympathetic. He asked me how much I owed Zalud and I told him it was about $22,000.

"Well, that isn't too much," he said to me. "Pay him the money and get on with your life."

It seemed that no avenue was open to me except to write this book, even without those few documents that Zalud still had.

By the end of January I'd received a Notice of Levy—Garnishment, from San Diego County Marshal. So once again, a lien was placed on my property, this time by my former attorney to get the fees he charged to supposedly represent us.

At least Elizabeth wasn't here to suffer this embarrassment again.

Five months later Zalud had all his money, and I never got any accounting of it all. Moreover, to this day Zalud's name still appears as lien holder against my property.

I remember soon after we hired Zalud and we were talking about being taken advantage of by Sessa and his attorneys. Zalud said to us that his uncle told him when he became an attorney that now he had a license to steal.

This should have raised my suspicions about him, but it didn't. Instead I had felt sorry for Zalud that his uncle would say such a thing.

Now I wonder just how much Zalud took his uncle's description to heart.

12
Final Appeal

I continued to write letters to plead my case, including another one to my congressman and another to the Bar, all to no avail. But, in the meantime, I was able to organize in my mind the convoluted events and begin to write them down for this book.

Also, my new attorney, Eugene P. Yale, wrote a letter to Zalud stating that Zalud had done a poor job of representing us and that he had failed to pursue the fraud aspect of our case which, if he had done so, would have probably resulted in us not having to pay the Sessas anything at all for the return of our Park.

Zalud answered him by letter saying, of course, that he'd got us our day in court and got us our Park back, his typical mantra. He even had the audacity to say that we could have spoken up before the judge when in fact that was not the case. Indeed, it was he who had told us before going in for the settlement hearing not to say anything to the judge and to just answer yes to his questions.

And what kind of questions were they, anyway? The judge never asked us to tell him in our own voices what happened. He knew everything he needed to know without us ever saying anything to him at all other than to answer yes or no as to whether we agreed to the settlement. Couldn't he see that there was something wrong? Shouldn't he have seen it?

Now I've always given my friends the benefit of the doubt. I'm loyal to them, and I feel it a sense of duty to honor them, as if I owe them for their trustworthiness. I've always felt it was a strength of mine, but it might also be a weakness.

It seems it might have been so with Paolo Sessa.

Of course, on occasion, everybody gets taken advantage of by trusting the wrong individuals, but I've never thought it worthwhile to be cynical. It always seemed better to see the good in one another than to be preoccupied with the bad.

But this experience with Sessa, Zalud and the justice system has worn on me.

How could Paolo Sessa have taken advantage of us so coldly? How could he have lied so easily to us, and right to our faces? Where was the honor in that? Where was the respect?

For me, honor, respect and trust came at an early age. My parents taught me right from wrong. They taught me when it was time to stand up for what I believed in and when it was time to give someone else a chance to do so.

And in school, I was taught about our system of justice. I was taught that the guilty would be found out and that the innocent would be shown to be innocent. Unfortunately, for me our justice system has not worked the way it was supposed to.

The truth is, there were a number of people in my past who instilled in me a sense of what is right, what is wrong, and what is truth. They helped to forge my character to the point that I have always demanded honesty from myself, even when others haven't. That is the way I was raised to behave.

As a result of these kinds of influences early on in life, I have become someone who, when a person acts in any kind way towards me, will go overboard to repay the kindness. It is just my personality. I have learned to trust people first, and sometimes it has gotten me into trouble.

In retrospect, this might have contributed to my being taken advantage of by Sessa.

But I wouldn't change most things that happened in my life as I did get to spend more than half a century with the sweetest person in the world, my dear late wife Elizabeth.

But I would give anything to have kept her from experiencing all of this. She didn't deserve it.

Elizabeth was the main person who influenced my character in a positive way. She was a model of honesty, integrity and trust, and her memory continues to comfort me when things get difficult.

But I miss her so, and I wish to God she hadn't had to go through all this.

I continue to try hard not to be embittered, but I confess I'm having difficulty doing so. In World War Two, I fought dictators and didn't let America down. I did my duty to help preserve this great nation and its laws, and I still feel that if I get the word out, as I have tried to do in this book, the American justice system will rectify the wrongs done to me.

But now, if the American justice system lets me down, I will be sorely tempted to have Elizabeth's body exhumed from the National Cemetery in Riverside and have it placed in a private cemetery, next to where I'll be eventually buried.

My heart chokes as I write these words. I want it to be true that Elizabeth and I were victims of unscrupulous people and some others who were misled or uninformed about our situation. But for those who knowingly did what they did, forgiveness will come hard.

I remember painfully how the despair slowly smothered the life out of my dear wife. I saw the despair grow in her face and take over her being.

I remember those weekly visits to the doctor and how in the hospital she refused to eat, upset still and disillusioned. She would make statements such as "Cruel world" and "I go in peace."

That was exceedingly unpleasant to hear, heart breaking.

Regardless, I would smile and say, "Honey, you have to eat."

And she would smile back at me and say, "Why?"

Then her smile would fade and she would repeat the words, "Corrupt judge, corrupt trial."

The nurses and staff were very nice with her, but you could see her desire to live was gone.

When the doctor came out of that room and told me that she had passed, I broke down. And then he told me that when she died, she was murmuring something about a trial.

I knew what those words were. I knew what her last thoughts in this world were about.

I was beside myself, all alone, my eyes gushing, driving home in tears. To this day I don't know how I made it. I remember thinking that now there was no one to turn to, and I had to make funeral arrangements by myself, broken hearted and in tears.

What a way to go out in this world—her last words: "Corrupt judge, corrupt trial."

In my grief and anger I told myself that those would be my last words, also.

So here I am, 85 years old and trying to find solace with this final appeal. Having no other recourse, I bring my case before you, the reader—the American public.

If nothing comes of writing this book, then so be it. At least I will have made the attempt. And if it brings me more strife, let me say that it will be nothing compared to what I've already gone through, as I've already lost the biggest part of me.

And if nothing else, the truth about what happened to us will be out there.

And I still believe in the truth, as did Elizabeth. God rest her soul.

Timeline of Documents

The following is a fairly complete listing of the numerous documents, legal and otherwise, relating to our case. Most notably missing are Elizabeth's and my depositions and Sessa's original lie-filled forensic accounting.

Of course, there may be other documents missing that I never knew about, documents that may possibly have been incriminating to the various parties involved. I feel that this may be so, but I'll leave it to the reader to decide.

If this listing had Elizabeth's and my depositions, a further look into the depth and degree of deception that Sessa and his attorneys were willing to sink would be illuminating.

For example, among the various and undated notes and papers that I have is one with the following: "Never received a copy of sale of our mobile home as Merrick promised."

This note to myself refers to what occurred when Sessa's attorney, Merrick, was interrogating me at my deposition. At one point Merrick held out a paper to me and asked if I'd ever seen it before, which of course I hadn't.

It was a paper that had no date, and it more or less stated in Sessa's handwriting that our mobile home was paid in full. Apparently, this was Sessa's way of proving that the money he was paying on the promissory note was actually for the sale of our mobile home.

Merrick held it out to me at my deposition. The short note concluded with something like "Mobile home paid in full."

I looked at him and said, " I've never seen this before."

"Well, you're seeing it now," he replied sarcastically.

The paper had no date on it and only Sessa's signature, not mine. I thought at the time that it would be a good piece of evidence to have when we went to trial, so I asked him for a copy.

"I'll see that you get a copy," Merrick replied quickly.

Looking back on it, I see now that by asking him to give me a copy, I might have been, in some subtle way, adding to the validity of the document, which I'm sure in retrospect is what Merrick wanted. Zalud never said a word in protest and I never received a copy.

This was just one incident that occurred. A full transcript of our depositions would show just how intimidating and rude Merrick was with us both and how little Zalud objected to our treatment.

There are also various letters to Sessa about the $400,000, notes to myself about the series of events, and lists of expenses, including the following:

STATUTES of LIMITATION
2. STATE-TAX IN LIMBO ?
$8,000 + $6,000 — 14,000.00
4. BACK HOE 6,000 + TO REPAIR — 10,000.00
5. SHREDDER — 1,000.00
3. COUNTY TAX ? — 12,456.84
6. ELECTRIC REBATE STATED WAS A LOSS — 10,000.00
7. NEGLECTED ROAD WORK — 1,500.00
8. NO PUMP IN ONE WELL — 500.00
9. PARK NOT IN COMPLIANCE WITH STATE GAS AUTHORITY — 10,000.00 +
83,456.84
10. ABSCOUNDED WITH ALL PAPERS PERTAINING TO PARK NO PINK SLIPS
$244,484.09 +

This is a list I made after I took over the Park again of the things that I felt Sessa owed me for, things that I already paid for, things that Sessa sold of mine that he shouldn't, and things that I would have to pay for due to his negligence.

The first item refers to the federal taxes I paid on the $400,000 portion of the selling price of the Park. The second refers to the state portion. Number three shows the state tax figures.

Number four is what I paid for the backhoe before I sold the Park to Sessa. While he owned the Park the backhoe broke down and he didn't fix it, but he did take out the motor, making it completely useless. Eventually, I heard from one of the persons that Sessa had got estimates and that he balked when he found out how much it would cost to repair, about $6000. To date, I have not repaired the machinery, but I have left it as is as physical evidence of Sessa's neglect and a symbol of the deteriorated condition of the Park after his stewardship.

Number five refers to the shredder, which is also now just a useless piece of machinery. In this case Sessa had the motor removed—a perfectly good motor this time, not one that needed repair—and drove off with it. I'm not sure if he sold the motor or not, though I suspect he did, but the shredder is now another symbol of Sessa's destructive years as owner of the Park.

Number six refers to what Sessa claimed was a loss on his electric bill while he owned the Park. This was actually a rebate by the electric company, though it was considered in the settlement as money Sessa paid out. As far as I know, Zalud said and did nothing about this blatant lie by Sessa.

Number seven refers to repairs I had to make on the road, which Sessa had left in disrepair while he owned the Park. Number eight refers to the pump that Sessa removed from one of the two wells at the Park. He had it removed, either to repair it or to sell it—again, I'm not sure—but either way I had to buy a new one when I got the Park back.

Number nine refers to the disrepair of the propane system and the amount that I had to pay to bring it into compliance. Number ten refers to the fact that Sessa took all the papers pertaining to the running of the Park—short-term and long-term leases, records of deposits made, etc. He started collecting deposits from the new tenants, something I had never done, and he didn't return the money to them or leave it for me to do so when the tenants later asked me for it.

He also took all the documents of ownership for the two trailers that belonged to the Park and the antique Studebaker truck that I included with the sale. He either sold or gave the truck to the Park worker, Martin Estrada, supposedly for $100 and possibly as compensation for work done. I have no idea what he did with it, but I know this for sure: that truck was worth thousands.

Sessa even took the historical documents that I had often thought I would donate to the Ramona Museum, papers dating back to the original owners, the Dukes. These papers are things that Sessa took that would have no value to him now at all, so I can only assume his intention was to leave me with nothing that was of any possible value to me or to the community, regardless if they had any value to him or not. The leases, of course, were documents that I sorely missed and that hampered my ability to carry on business.

There are many other such notes and papers that I won't include in the following listing, but that were helpful to my reconstructing the series of events.

Also, I've noted in the timeline certain events that occurred for which I have no document, but that are of some importance to seeing the whole picture.

For convenience sake, I've divided this timeline of documents into sections roughly corresponding to the chapters in this book.

Chapter 2
Our Mobile Home Park

September 19, 1969

Escrow statement, to Mike and Elizabeth for $120,000.

— This was not the total price we paid for the RMHP. The down payment was a property we had in Las Vegas worth approximately $100,000. And we also gave the Mersmans about $25,000 and we paid all the fees, including escrow. The total figure was approximately $230,000.

This seems to be appropriate for the time and the figure of $900,000 is appropriate for 1992. In fact, an independent broker offered us $850,000 for the Park in 1991.

We weren't interested in selling the place at the time, but it gave us a starting point when we did sell to Sessa. The broker just knew us through the WMA, Western Mobile-home Association, and he contacted us from time to time unsolicited. His offer increased each time we talked.

Chapter 4
Blind Trust

September 18, 1992

Standard form showing $500,000 and two payments of $100,000, one labeled "to seller out of escrow" and with a balance of $300,000 payable at $2500/month.

— This was a preliminary document that Sessa showed us just to give us an idea of what the figures would be, or at least that's what he said after my protests. It shows us receiving two payments of $100,000, but no mention of the other $400,000 that we would be paid. The final figure on these preliminary papers show $300,000 as the amount we would carry on the official loan. Of course, the figures didn't jibe, but he assured me it would all show correctly on the final papers.

In retrospect, I should have realized that Sessa was already throwing confusion into the process, confusion that he would carry through to the later trial case and that may have eventually infused every participant.

September 30, 1992

Certificate of release of buyer from previous debts owed by Ceperichs and RMHP.

— We had no leans, no tax back payments or any encumbrances.

October 2, 1992

Escrow papers, including Closing Statement dated October 30 totaling $502,200 and showing initial $100,000 payment.

— This was the one we signed. Of course, it didn't say anything about the other $400,000 or the other $100,000 down payment.

Sessa did represent to me that he had the down payments, both of them, in cash in the bank, but I later learned that he had to borrow the first down payment from the bank and, of course, he never did give me the second one out of escrow. I found this out when I saw his bank statements among the papers that Zalud showed me during the trial process.

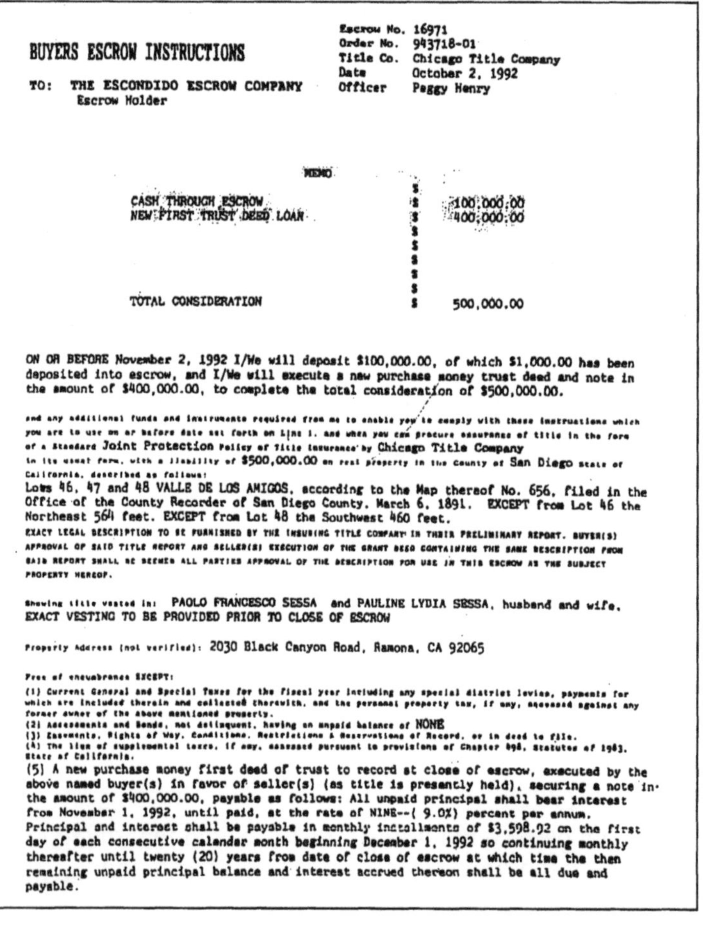

BUYERS ESCROW INSTRUCTIONS

TO: THE ESCONDIDO ESCROW COMPANY
Escrow Holder

Escrow No. 16971
Order No. 943718-01
Title Co. Chicago Title Company
Date October 2, 1992
Officer Peggy Henry

MEMO

CASH THROUGH ESCROW	$	100,000.00
NEW FIRST TRUST DEED LOAN	$	400,000.00
TOTAL CONSIDERATION	$	500,000.00

ON OR BEFORE November 2, 1992 I/We will deposit $100,000.00, of which $1,000.00 has been deposited into escrow, and I/We will execute a new purchase money trust deed and note in the amount of $400,000.00, to complete the total consideration of $500,000.00.

and any additional funds and instruments required from me to enable you to comply with these instructions which you are to use on or before date set forth on Line 1, and when you can procure assurance of title in the form of a Standard Joint Protection Policy of Title Insurance by Chicago Title Company in its usual form, with a liability of $500,000.00 on real property in the County of San Diego State of California, described as follows:

Lots 46, 47 and 48 VALLE DE LOS AMIGOS, according to the Map thereof No. 656, filed in the Office of the County Recorder of San Diego County, March 6, 1891. EXCEPT from Lot 46 the Northeast 564 feet. EXCEPT from Lot 48 the Southwest 460 feet.

EXACT LEGAL DESCRIPTION TO BE FURNISHED BY THE INSURING TITLE COMPANY IN THEIR PRELIMINARY REPORT. BUYER(S) APPROVAL OF SAID TITLE REPORT AND SELLER(S) EXECUTION OF THE GRANT DEED CONTAINING THE SAME DESCRIPTION FROM SAID REPORT SHALL BE DEEMED ALL PARTIES APPROVAL OF THE DESCRIPTION FOR USE IN THIS ESCROW AS THE SUBJECT PROPERTY HEREOF.

Showing title vested in: PAOLO FRANCESCO SESSA and PAULINE LYDIA SESSA, husband and wife. EXACT VESTING TO BE PROVIDED PRIOR TO CLOSE OF ESCROW

Property Address (not verified): 2030 Black Canyon Road, Ramona, CA 92065

Free of encumbrances EXCEPT:

(1) Current General and Special Taxes for the fiscal year including any special district levies, payments for which are included therein and collected therewith, and the personal property tax, if any, assessed against any former owner of the above mentioned property.
(2) Assessments and Bonds, not delinquent, having an unpaid balance of NONE
(3) Easements, Rights of Way, Conditions, Restrictions & Reservations of Record, or in deed to file.
(4) The lien of supplemental taxes, if any, assessed pursuant to provisions of Chapter 498, Statutes of 1983, State of California.
(5) A new purchase money first deed of trust to record at close of escrow, executed by the above named buyer(s) in favor of seller(s) (as title is presently held), securing a note in the amount of $400,000.00, payable as follows: All unpaid principal shall bear interest from November 1, 1992, until paid, at the rate of NINE--(9.0%) percent per annum. Principal and interest shall be payable in monthly installments of $3,598.92 on the first day of each consecutive calendar month beginning December 1, 1992 so continuing monthly thereafter until twenty (20) years from date of close of escrow at which time the then remaining unpaid principal balance and interest accrued thereon shall be all due and payable.

October 16, 1992

Trust deed note for $400,000 at 9% ($3598.92/month).

— This was the note attached to the above-the-table transaction after the $100,000 downpayment.

October 20, 1992

Lenders loss payable endorsement (insurance?).

—When Sessa switched insurance, his new company asked if there was any lien holder on the property. He said there wasn't, but there actually was, us, and it was important to show as much.

This was brought to our attention by my original insurance carrier, and we then called Sessa's new company and told them we were the lien holders, and they put us down as such.

Sessa was obviously misrepresenting the issue because he'd be the first to get paid in case of a claim.

Also, in retrospect, this seems an obvious attempt to set down a false paper trail, one that would help to obfuscate matters legally. From the start, his intentions were less than honorable.

October 22, 1992

Signed over Grant Deed.

— We possibly did this at the escrow office at the same time, or it was sent to us and we signed it after they did a title search.

October 28, 1992

Certificate of insurance in Sessas' names.

— This one shows us as lien holders. This was one lie that Sessa didn't get away with.

November 1, 1992

Promissory note for $400,000 at 0% ($1500/month) for two years only. After that the interest would be 9%.

— Sessa brought this to us and I asked him again for $100,000, but he said he didn't have it.

"But you promised me you'd give it to me," I said, and I told him I needed it in order to buy the modular home.

"Mike," Sessa said, "I'd give it to you, but I don't have it. If I had it, I'd give it to you."

He never did say when he'd have it for me, and there was no mention of the downpayment in the document, but what could I do? At least we now had a signed paper for the other $400,000 of the selling price.

November 6, 1992, et al.

Various checks to Martin Estrada, the worker at the Park.

— I was giving Martin $10/week extra as a raise, and I told Sessa about this. But he didn't show that he was paying Martin this extra $520/year. Instead he showed it as paying Estrada's wife to clean the coach in space #2.

Later, at his deposition, Sessa claimed this as an expense rather than as normal payment of Estrada's wages.

Also, he didn't pay this to Estrada immediately. It was only after Estrada complained to Sessa and asked him for the money that Sessa gave him a check for one year for the $520.

So Sessa lied in his deposition.

November 25, 1992

Letter from Clement W. Morin, CPA, stating the required 4th quarter estimates for federal and state taxes.

— Morin was our accountant.

March 19 & April 9, 1993

Checks from Sessas to Mike for repairs and parts. March 19 ($515.22) is to Mike signed by Pauline Sessa for repair of the pump and back hoe; April 9 ($500) is to Mike signed by Pauline Sessa for parts.

— These are for things at the Park, but not a fee for managing the Park, which we were doing for almost a year and a half.

Sessa was compensated for 46 months by Judge Hollywood, but actually we managed the place for 18 of those months.

In fact, it was discussed and admitted to openly that we were the managers, but for only 6 months, and we never got compensated for even that in the final judgment.

We did a fair job of managing it for the 6 months, at least, before we backed off somewhat.

September 21, 1993

Strategic Mortgage Services (SMS) letter asking for verification of Sessa loan.

— The Sessas were trying to get a loan, maybe to buy other property. Elizabeth called them on this one.

March 1994

I approached Sessa and asked him again for the $100,000 down payment he that owed us on the $4000,000 promissory note, and I gave him a document that showed he now owed me for interest on that amount, since he had refused to stand by the agreement on the $100,000 downpayment.

The interest on this $100,000, verified by my banker, came to about $37,000. I figured I'd already given him the whole $400,000 interest free for nearly two years, and that was enough. If he wasn't going to give me the down payment as agreed, then he was going to have to pay me interest on the amount. After all, it had now been almost a year and a half since escrow, a year and a half since he was supposed to give us the money.

He said that if he showed this document to his wife, she'd have a heart attack, and he walked off. He later came back to me and threatened, "I'll fix you."

Sessa talked about his wife having a heart attack, but in reality it was Elizabeth's health that was deteriorating. Her blood pressure had increased, as had mine, and though hers was only a little elevated before all this, I had never had high blood pressure before.

I was in my late 70s and had never had high blood pressure before this time. Elizabeth had been taking one pill for high blood pressure, which started about the time when we sold the Park, but after all these problems with the Sessas, she had to take two pills. I remember her saying to me that she wished we'd never met these people.

April 4, 1994

First letter to Sessa about the $100,000 down payment.

— Since we were no longer speaking to him, not even when he picked up the monthly rent for our mobile home space, we brought the issue up through this certified letter.

My wife wrote the letter and I signed it. Sessa never responded to it.

May 10, 1994

Ceperichs as credit references for Sessa.

— I refused to sign it.

May 16, 1994

Letter from Strategic Mortgage Services (SMS) to verify Sessa loan. SMS was "developing a Mortgage Report on [Sessas]."

— I refused to verify as I wasn't sure if I'd be responsible for his loan if he defaulted. Besides, by this time we didn't trust him at all anymore.

Possibly, Sessa felt that he wasn't going to be able to take us for much longer and he was trying to get a loan with our verification before things between us got even worse.

May 16, 1994

Request for verification of rent or mortgage account.

— After we refused to verify for this loan, things broke down completely. From this point on, the relationship was nil.

We never talked to Sessa again, but we did correspond by mail, telling him that we were going to close the right of way to go to our other property where we were building our modular home. This easement was also used to get to an area of the RMHP, so when we threatened to fence it off because he was not helping to maintain it as he agreed, Sessa was angered and, possibly, started to concoct a case against us.

May 18,1994

Well permit for our modular home.

August 2, 1994

Second letter to Sessa about the $100,000 down payment.

— He never replied to either of our letters.

September 19, 1994

County Health permit and plans to build a septic system for our modular home.

— We were continuing to proceed with our plans even though Sessa was soon to stop paying us the $1500.

November 1, 1994

Sessa didn't pay the $1500 payment on the promissory note, and I would have confronted him when he came to collect the rent as he usually did, but he didn't come for it that month.

We had been taking out our rent and utilities from the $1500 payment he was making, and he would pay us the difference. This always occurred at the first of the month and it was always done in cash.

We were getting close to closing the deal for our modular home. We had been shopping around for the right one, dealing with permits, etc., so we didn't pursue why Sessa hadn't paid us. We had enough to think about, and we figured we'd just have to take him to small claims court when and if the amount got to $5000.

In the meantime, we would have moved away from the Park and been rid of Sessa's influence, to a certain extent, if we could have afforded to. Indeed, if he'd paid us the second $100,000 downpayment, we'd have been already gone.

Chapter 5
Small Claims

January 19, 1995

Letter from Sessa claiming that Ceperichs owe back rent for the past 3 months totaling $1169.58 and that, as of October 1, 1994, the mobile home in space #18 is paid off, and if the Ceperichs want to stay in that mobile home, they have to start paying $700/month plus $30/month for the garage.

Other stipulations were listed, including to return the keys, stop stealing materials and equipment, and sign and mail to Sessa the title of the mobile home as being paid in full.

— We didn't owe any back rent, and Sessa lied and used the payment on the promissory note as if it were for the mobile home. There was no agreement as to how long we could stay in our own mobile home, and we were paying rent the whole time, and it wasn't even discounted.

We did pay only for utilities for the first 6 months, but then we started paying rent as did everybody else staying at the Park. So the figure for back rent makes no sense at all.

Moreover, his statement that he had paid us off for our mobile home was a scam on his part to cover his paying us on the promissory note. As for the garage fee, we agreed that we didn't have to pay for storage until we got our new home built, so he was also reneging on that promise to us, as well.

As to the keys, they were in the office the whole time so we weren't keeping them from him. As to the materials and equipment, we only used what was ours, so he was again lying.

January 20, 1995

Small claims papers for $5000 for stolen "materials, equipment, tools & other things."

— This made us both very upset, especially since it was all lies. And it was more than a simple diversion for us. Our lives came practically to a stop, not to mention that we both became mistrusting. We became very cautious with others, not just the

Sessas. I realize now just how much all of this affected our view toward others and life itself.

We prepared for the court date. Sciarretta had pictures taken and advised me what to do. We also decided to contact our accountant Clement Morin and tell him about the "deal" with Sessa to keep $400,000 of the selling price under the table. Of course, he told me that we shouldn't have tried to save taxes in this way and he filed an amended return for the year we sold the property.

I ended up paying $24,000 in back taxes, and this was on money that we either didn't get, if you consider the $100,000 out of escrow payment, or money that Sessa now claimed was for payment for our mobile home and not for the $400,000 portion of the total selling price.

February 17, 1995

Small claims judgment for defendant M. Ceperich: "Defendant does not owe plaintiff any money on plaintiff's claim."

— Judge Margaret Riggs heard the case. Sessa spoke first. And this is verbatim:

"This Mike Ceperich is no good. He steals everything."

But he never produced any evidence. Instead he immediately pulled out the promissory note and said, "Furthermore, Your Honor, this document is no good. It's the same as the other one."

The bailiff took the document to the judge, who looked at it and said to Sessa, "This looks good to me. You signed it."

She then handed it back to the bailiff to show to both of us to confirm that we'd both signed it, and we both said that we had, including Sessa. The bailiff took the document back to the judge and she took it and said she'd render her decision. Sessa thanked her three times, each one louder than the other.

The case was supposed to be for stolen things, but Sessa made no mention of these stolen items. He went instead, almost immediately, to trying to get the promissory note disqualified.

He obviously had that in mind all along. The stolen items were just a pretext for doing so.

February 23, 1995

Fire marshal inspection of access road for our modular home property.

— We moved in around this time. We looked for and bought our home in late 1994, and it was moved onto our property sometime around the end of November of 1994.

March 1, 1995

We received in the mail Judge Riggs' decision in our favor. We didn't owe Sessa anything.

We were both relieved, but we took it more or less in stride, as we still didn't have the money Sessa owed us. We did think that this might have been a turning point and that we might be, eventually, receiving the money on the promissory note.

We even took the document to City Hall to record it with the county. Thus did it become a matter of record with both the county and the small claims court records. Now that we knew that Sessa was trying to get out of the agreement completely, we felt this action necessary.

We didn't talk to Sessa.

March 8, 1995

Final document of fire Marshall approval and county planning department for approval of foundation for our modular home. This was the final inspection.

April 15, 1995

Sessa tax return showing net loss of $61,881.

— This came out in court later. We'd always shown a profit running the Park and it was obvious that Sessa was being fraudulent with his tax returns.

He later admitted to Zalud, our attorney, that he had made $174,000 in profit over the 46 months he had the Park.

April 17, 1995

Letter to Mr. Pfingst, DA, claiming fraud by the Sessas and offering to bring in all the papers for review.

April 19,1995

Letter from Barbara J. Hall, Supv. Investigative Specialist...

April 20, 1995

... at the District Attorney's Fraud Division, asking for all the pertinent details and documents of the case.

Chapter 6
2.3 Million!

April 20, 1995

Complaint for preliminary injunction from Walters, actually by Julie Ann Bowler for Walters.

Also, a letter and temporary restraining order from Walters to Joseph A. Sciarretta, Attorney at Law.

Also, declarations of Julie Ann Bowler, attorney, and Debbie Ayles, paralegal, in support of ex-parte application for temporary restraining order.

— We were shocked that Sessa had got Walters as an attorney. We knew Walters. He was involved with the Western Mobilehome Association (WMA) and I had even got his help in a few legal matters. So, at one time he had represented us, and now he was representing Sessa.

Sciarretta had helped us prepare for the small claims action, and we retained him to deal with this.

April 21, 1995

A second and mistaken letter sent by Barbara Hall regretfully declaring that after reviewing the facts (which they could not possibly have yet received) there was no basis for further action. On this letter a handwritten note in Elizabeth's hand.

Also, from Walters to Sciarretta: "Enclosed for your review is the Order regarding the ex-parte hearing..." and an order to appear in court on May 5, 1995.

Also, from Walters and Bowler, Declaration of Paolo Sessa in support of Ex-Parte Application for Temporary Restraining order & Order to Show Cause Re: Preliminary Injunction. An early succinct statement by Sessa.

April 24, 1995

Follow-up letter from Elizabeth to the District Attorney briefly stating facts about fraud and enclosing copies of the two notes totaling $900,000.

April 26, 1995

Julie Ann Bowler's Plaintiff's Notice of Lodgment (list of exhibits).

— This was sent to Sciarretta and claimed that we were committing fraud, etc. In essence, Sessa was accusing us of the very things he was guilty of.

Sciarretta then contacted me to ask for an $8000 retainer to fight the case. I asked him for a week or 10 days to get the money together, but he then refused to take the case and gave me back all my papers and pertinent documents.

May 4, 1995

County health services notice of violation, failing septic system.

— It was raining at the time and the tanks overflowed. I knew what to do, but we weren't there during that period, and I doubt Sessa would have asked me for advice anyway, given all that was happening.

This is something I would have taken care of easily, even during the 16 months we managed the place for him, and despite what had happened between us, I'd have told him what to do had he asked me. This shows how incapable he was to handle the managing of the RMHP.

May 5, 1995

Notice of case assignment, signed by Debbie Ayles and dated April 27, 1995.

— This was when the local real estate broker told us about Zalud, and we retained him to handle the case.

May 6, 1995

Letter from Zalud to Ceperichs thanking them for their business and setting down the fee agreement.

May 16,1995

We appealed to the State of California, Business, Transportation and Housing Agency and received this letter from them:

STATE OF CALIFORNIA — BUSINESS, TRANSPORTATION AND HOUSING AGENCY PETE WILSON, Gov

DEPARTMENT OF REAL ESTATE
1350 Front Street, Room 3064
San Diego, California 92101
(619) 525-4192

May 16, 1995

Mr. & Mrs. Michael Mark Ceperich
2030-18 Black Canyon Road
Ramona, CA 92065

Re: Paolo Sessa, PC #395-0515-002

Dear Mr. & Mrs. Ceperich:

I am in receipt of your complaint dated May 4, 1995, where you explained you sold your mobile home park to Paolo and Pauline Sessa during September, 1992. The sales price was $[illegible]00,000 with you carrying a $400,000 first trust deed at [illegible] interest. A $400,000 second deed of trust was executed in your favor, to evidence the interest on the first trust deed. [illegible] the Sessa s are [illegible] paying the note.

Based upon the information you provided we will not be able to intercede on your behalf as we lack sufficient grounds to do so. It appears the underlying basis of your complaint is a contractual dispute or a breech of contract that is outside of the Real Estate Commissioner's jurisdiction. As you have retained attorney Kenneth J. Zalud to represent you, Mr. Zalud should advise you how to proceed with your civil action.

I'm sorry we could not be of service; however, we will retain your complaint for three years should it have bearing on future activities of Mr. or Mrs. Sessa.

Thank you for writing.

Respectfully,

J. CHRIS GRAVES
Managing Deputy Commissioner II

JCG:lm

Obviously we had not been clear enough, so we wrote another letter correcting the mistakes and explaining how Sessa portrayed himself as knowledgeable in real estate matters, calling the promissory note a blind trust and telling us what "smart people" do to save money on taxes. We argued that he had misrepresented himself, and his true intention was to defraud us of hundreds of thousands of dollars.

Can you see how extensive our search was to get justice? Can you imagine how much energy and time this took from us as well? And more and more, we were being swayed into putting our trust in Zalud as our only way out of this mess.

May 19, 1995

Last two pages (5 & 6) of Zalud's argument as to why "the conduct of the Ceperichs need not be controlled until the pending 'companion' litigation is resolved."

— Zalud was successful and the restraining order that was to keep me from accessing and using my own tools was set aside.

At the time, Sessa had even told a friend of mine to leave the Park, a person who I discovered also knew Sessa. This person explained that Sessa and he had had a run in and that he was keenly aware of Sessa's demeanor and capacity for wrongdoing.

I suppose Sessa didn't want my friend to expose him for who he was, so he told my friend to leave and never come back.

May 23, 1995

Letter to District Attorney's Fraud Division.

— They were sympathetic but said they couldn't do anything and that we should pursue the matter in court. More and more it was looking as if our day in court was to be our one and only chance for justice.

In our subsequent meetings with Zalud, it was agreed that a jury trial was best if we were to expose Sessa for what he was.

Elizabeth and I talked often about this and we prepared ourselves to go before our peers and plead our case. We were sure that a jury of our peers would see how Sessa had taken advantage of us with his lies and subterfuge.

Though we felt a little better about taking hold of things and defending ourselves, it was still a pressure-filled time for us both. The shock of the reality of our situation had already set in and passed somewhat, but we were nonetheless still overcome with worry and grief and we often lost sleep over it.

May 26, 1995

Zalud enters into evidence the handwritten memorandum of the $900,000 offer, $400,000 promissory note and accompanying security agreement, and small claims court claim and judgment in favor of Michael Ceperich.

May 26, 1995

We sent a letter off to the State Department of Real Estate with the explanations they asked for and got a quick reply, but it only again directed us back to our attorney for advice.

STATE OF CALIFORNIA — BUSINESS, TRANSPORTATION AND HOUSING AGENCY PETE WILSON, *Governor*

DEPARTMENT OF REAL ESTATE
1350 Front Street, Room 3064
San Diego, California 92101
(619) 525-4192

May 26, 1995

Mr. Michael Ceperich
2030-18 Black Canyon Road
Ramona, CA 92065

Re: Paolo Sessa, PC #395-0515-002

Dear Mr. Ceperich:

Thank you for your follow up letter dated May 22, 1995, wherein you provided additional information regarding your complaint with Paolo and Pauline Sessa's handling the sale of your mobile home park in Ramona, California.

I reviewed your letter with attachments along with the original package you submitted. Though I believe I understand the problem you face, I am unable to cite a specific real estate law violation that could be used to discipline Mr. or Mrs. Sessa. It appears your attorney, Mr. Zalud, should be consulted for his suggestions on your next step.

Regretfully we can be of no further service.

Sincerely,

J. Chris Graves

J. CHRIS GRAVES
Managing Deputy Commissioner II

We were trying to bring to light Sessa's lies about having much experience in real estate. We figured they might at least chastise him somehow, but again, our only recourse was through the courts with Zalud.

DUNCAN HUNTER

CHAIRMAN
REPUBLICAN RESEARCH COMMITTEE

COMMITTEE ON ARMED SERVICES

SEAPOWER
RESEARCH AND DEVELOPMENT

REPUBLICAN TASK FORCE ON AGRICULTURE

The 103d Congress
U.S. House of Representatives
Washington, DC 20515-0552

AUTHORIZATION FORM

THE PRIVACY ACT OF 1974 (PL 93-579) BECAME FULLY EFFECTIVE ON SEPTEMBER 7, 1975. THE PURPOSE OF THIS ACT IS TO CONTROL THE FEDERAL GOVERNMENT'S COLLECTION AND DISSEMINATION OF PERSONAL INFORMATION ABOUT INDIVIDUAL CITIZENS. ONE OF THE PROVISIONS OF THE ACT PROHIBITS THE FEDERAL GOVERNMENT FROM REVEALING ANY INFORMATION FROM ANY CITIZEN'S GOVERNMENTAL RECORDS WITHOUT THE EXPRESS PERMISSION OF THE PERSON INVOLVED. THE PRIVACY ACT DOES NOT AUTHORIZE THE DISCLOSURE OF RECORDS TO MEMBERS OF CONGRESS ACTING IN THEIR INDIVIDUAL CAPACITIES OR ON BEHALF OF THEIR CONSTITUENTS, UNLESS THE INDIVIDUAL TO WHOM THE RECORDS PERTAIN HAS CONSENTED.

I HEREBY AUTHORIZE CONGRESSMAN DUNCAN HUNTER OR A MEMBER OF HIS STAFF TO MAKE THE APPROPRIATE INQUIRY ON MY BEHALF.

NAME: MRS. & MR. MICHAEL CEPERICH

ADDRESS: 2030 BLACK CANYON RD.
RAMONA, CA. 92065

PHONE: (HOME) (619) 788-7333 (WORK) ______ SSN 312-09-3944

CLAIM NUMBER ______ OTHER ______

PLEASE EXPLAIN IN YOUR OWN WORDS: WE, MICHAEL & ELIZABETH CEPERICH ARE OLDER SENIOR CITIZENS AND ARE VICTIMS OF A SCAM, PERPETRATED BY MR. PAOLO & PAULINE SESSA. (REAL ESTATE AGENTS) PERHAPS YOU CAN INTERCEDE IN ASSISTING US THROUGH THE VETERANS ADMINISTRATION. THE SESSA'S APPROACHED US IN THE YEAR OF 1989 LOOKING FOR A MOBILEHOME PARK TO PURCHASE, OURS BEING RAMONA MOBILE PARK. FINALLY AFTER MANY VISITS TO THE PARK WE DECIDED TO SELL TO THE SESSA'S IN 1992. IN PREPARATION FOR ESCROW ALL THE IMPUT FOR ESCROW WAS MADE BY THE SESSA'S. THE SALE OF THE PARK WAS $ 900,000.00. $500,000.00 WAS NEGOTIATED IN ESCROW AS PART OF THE SALE. $100,000.00 WAS PAID IN ESCROW AND $100,000.00 WAS TO BE PAID

SIGNATURE: Michael Ceperich DATE: 6 - 1 - 1995
PLEASE USE OTHER SIDE IF MORE SPACE IS REQUIRED

June 1, 1995

Letter to our congressman, Duncan Hunter.

Second page of Duncan Hunter letter.

AT CLOSE OF ESCROW, THIS AMOUNT WAS NEVER PAID. A PROMISSARY NOTE, OUT OF ESCROW FOR $ 400,000.00 WAS PART OF THE CONTRACT TO BE PAID AT $ 1,000.00 [handwritten: 5] PER MONTH, [handwritten: FOR TWO YEARS.] NO INTEREST. ANOTHER NOTE WAS MADE TO COVER INTEREST FOR THE PROMISSORY NOTE FOR $ 400,000.00. MONTHLY PAYMENTS WERE TO BE MADE FOR $ 1,500.00 PLUS BALLOON PAYMENTS AFTER RETIRING IN TWO YEARS. THE SESSA'S ARE ALLEGING THAT THE $1,500.00 PAYMENTS ON THE PROMISSORY NOTE WAS TO PURCHASE OUR MOBILEHOME, THIS IS NOT TRUE. WE NEVER AGREED VERBALLY OR BY CONTRACT WHICH THEY STATED THEY POSSESS. NO PAYMENTS ARE FORTHCOMING ON THE PROMISSORY NOTE, LIKEWISE NO MONIES ARE BEING PAID ON THE INTEREST NOTE. MR. SESSA STATED THE REASON FOR MAKING THIS CONTRACT THIS WAY WAS THAT THE GOVERNMENT GETS TOO MUCH MONEY. HE TOLD US THIS IS LEGAL, GOES ON ALL THE TIME AND IS CALLED A BLIND TRUST. WE TOLD MR. SESSA WE NEVER HEARD OF A BLIND TRUST. I SUGGESTED WE GO TO AN ATTORNEY, HE STATED IT IS A WASTE OF MONEY, WE KNOW AS MUCH AS THE ATTORNEYS. NOW WE REALIZE THE SESSA'S WERE NOT TRUSTWORTHY AND THEIR INTENT WAS TO DEFRAUD. THUS FAR THE SESSA'S OWE US APPROXIMATELY $159,000.00 PLUS.

Also, Notice of suit from R. Michael Walters, Walters & Ward, and a Summons, a long document containing a confusing breakdown of the pecuniary amounts ("2.3 Million").

— This amount was a big shock. We weren't sophisticated enough to realize at the time that this was part of Sessa's modus operandi, to scare us into submission, or worse. Sessa knew that this type of action would have some bad effect on our health.

Indeed, my wife and I lost even more sleep after this, staying up late into the night and talking about how our lives were turned asunder, how such a thing could have happened to us, and how much we wished we'd never met the Sessas.

How could someone be so unscrupulous and lie and betray our friendship, which we were so open and willing to offer?

We were now more upset than ever and it showed on us both. Our lives were more than ever imbued with this unpleasantness. We stopped going out at all, lost our appetites and even lost our feeling for others to some extent. We started to feel we couldn't trust anyone anymore, and it showed in our relationships with friends, even though we were cautious enough to keep what was happening to us to ourselves for the most part. After all, it was exceedingly embarrassing to us that we had been suckered into this so deeply.

In retrospect, it might have been better if we had shared it, but indeed, it was devastating to have it be later exposed to all our tenants and friends publicly. I remember Elizabeth crying when the marshals came out to administer the lien. I'm crying now as I write this. I was becoming very concerned for Elizabeth's health. She was so hurt by all of this.

Zalud had little to say about the amount. He simply stated that we could live with ourselves, never mentioned any amount that we might be able to get from Sessa, and restated that we were going to get him.

I tried as best I could to maintain a strong front for Elizabeth. I even wrote another letter to our US congressman, bringing up that I was a veteran and could he please contact the veterans administration for help. I was desperate. But the man from the veterans administration told me on the phone that they didn't get into legal matters.

June 16, 1995

Letter from Duncan Hunter, Member of Congress, stating that a letter was sent on Mike's behalf to the Department of Veterans Affairs, whose response was negative.

June 25, 1995

Check from Sessa for $12,000 for back payment of $1500 per month payments on promissory note.

— Evidently, Sessa's attorney had advised him that he'd have to continue the payments on the promissory note. When I told Zalud I got the check, he told me, for the first time, not to cash it.

June 26, 1995

Walters' Notice of Amount of General & Specific Damages Sought Pursuant to Local Rule 10.4(b)(2). Many monetary and pecuniary figures mentioned.

June 30, 1995

Received check for $12,000 from Sessa as back payment on the promissory note (see page 48).

July 5, 1995

Letter from Zalud to R. Michael Walters, Walters & Ward, about Sessa's amended complaint and resumed payments on the promissory note.

Also, letter from Zalud to Ceperichs (shown on page 49).

— I'm still puzzled as to why Zalud told us not cash the check. I remember asking him why a copy of the check wouldn't be evidence enough, but he told me again, in person, that we should keep the original checks. He also told me not to cash the $1500 checks when they resumed. We complied.

I had already started to question Zalud's actions, but Elizabeth had been more patient with him, and she still was, even with this, and I went along with her judgment. Thinking back on it, he was probably doing the right thing generally, but I still don't understand the check business. At least we'd have had that money to use toward our new home.

But also thinking back, had I cashed these checks, they would not have been taken into account in the final settlement and I might not have agreed to that settlement at the higher figure.

Moreover, why would Zalud instruct us not even to open the envelopes that the checks arrived in? How would I know what they were if I didn't open the envelopes to see what was inside?

Indeed, I did open the envelopes, but I did not cash the checks. When I informed him that I got the $12,000 check and that I knew I did because I opened it, he said nothing about not opening the envelop, but he reminded me not to cash it.

July 7, 1995

Photocopy of check from Sessa for continued monthly payment on the promissory note.

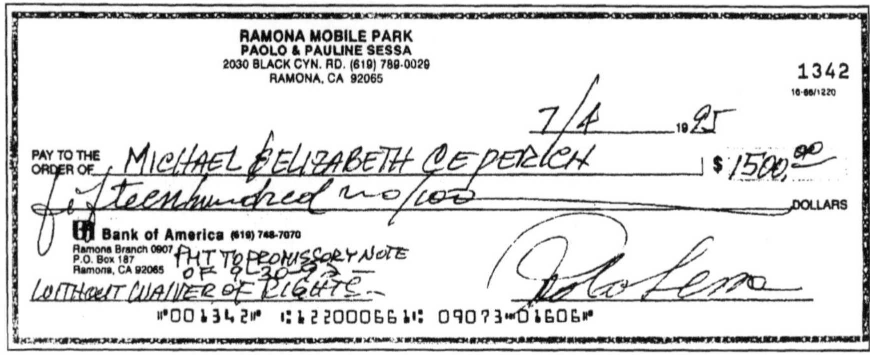

RAMONA MOBILE PARK
PAOLO & PAULINE SESSA
2030 BLACK CYN. RD. (619) 789-0029
RAMONA, CA 92065

1342
16-66/1220

7/4 19 95

PAY TO THE ORDER OF Michael Elizabeth Ceperich $ 1500.00

fifteenhundred no/100 DOLLARS

Bank of America (619) 748-7070
Ramona Branch 0907
P.O. Box 187
Ramona, CA 92065

PMT TO PROMISSORY NOTE OF 9-30-93
WITHOUT WAIVER OF RIGHTS

Paolo Sessa

⑈001342⑈ ⑆122000661⑆ 09073⑈01606⑈

July 21, 1995

Letter to Duncan Hunter asking him to set up an audience with DA Paul Pfingst concerning fraud of seniors.

— Though Elizabeth was patient with Zalud and things seemed to be turning around generally, she agreed that informing our congressman about our predicament and asking for more help was not inappropriate.

What gave us the idea was seeing DA Pfingst on television stating that he was going to pursue fraud against senior citizens. We called first and wrote a letter to Pfingst, but got no response, so we decided to contact Hunter, who eventually wrote us a letter stating that his office had sent a letter to Pfingst to get in touch with us and possibly intervene on our behalf.

The DA never contacted us.

September 13, 1995

Filing date for Substitution of Attorney, N. Munro Merrick for R. Michael Walters. Signed by attorneys on August 24, and by Sessas on August 31.

— We were originally told this by Zalud, who went on to say that Merrick was "good buddies" with Judge Hollywood. He said little else and I don't remember how he characterized the progress of the case or if he made a characterization at all. I only remember him insisting, often and repeatedly, that we were going to get Sessa good.

Also, at this point we started going to court once a week, on Fridays.

September 21, 1995

Messenger service form for delivered documents, handwritten and hard to read.

— I believe these were forms asking for our personal information, Elizabeth's and mine.

But also, with the change of attorney, Sessa began again to claim that the selling price of the Park was only $500,000. I questioned Zalud about this and he just said that Sessa was getting himself in deeper by lying through his teeth.

October 26, 1995

Form interrogatories from Merrick: one for Mike and one for Elizabeth.

— Though these were forms, the questions were still intrusive and troubling for two people our age.

October 27, 1995

Zalud's Reply Memorandum of Points and Authorities in Support of Motion for Summary Adjudication.

— This contained some good points made for our case, and Zalud was happy about it.

November 8, 1995

Request from Merrick for income and expense statements and balance sheets for the Park, 1990-92; "All evidence supporting your contention as stated in paragraph 5 of your Cross-Complaint, that 'at the insistence of the Cross-Defendants,' you 'agreed to and allowed the escrow to reflect only a portion of the true sales price.'"

Also, a set of requests for Elizabeth.

Also, a few interrogatories for Elizabeth.

Also, an undated request for admissions that the Sessas have made all payments of both notes.

December 19, 1995

Elizabeth's response to interrogatories.

Elizabeth's response to requests.

Mike's response to requests, but not to interrogatories.

— This was a fine way to spend our holidays.

December 25, 1995

It was a sad Christmas.

January 17, 1996

Proof of service by mail to Merrick, an expert witness list and declaration.

— I never got any input from Zalud as to who these witnesses were.

January 26, 1996

Form interrogatories for Sessa from Zalud.

Also, same for Sessa's wife.

Also, Zalud to Merrick, Demand for Production by Sessa.

February 14, 1996

Sessa's response to "Demand for Production" showing a number of objections.

February 20, 1996

Letter from Zalud to Manny Gonzales apologizing for confusion and enclosing "the requisite retainer check" and "the two primary documents we claim were drafted by the defendant."

— This visit was in early February, before Elizabeth's deposition.

Gonzales was the carbon tester of the handwritten note by Sessa stating $900,000 as the selling price. Zalud took us to his office someplace in San Diego. We took the one document with us on that day, so I am not sure what "two primary documents" Zalud is talking about here. The second one, I believe, was the one with the Xed out sections, one of the first papers Sessa showed us before we went to escrow. It showed a $500,000 figure, but it also showed a second downpayment, the one out of escrow.

I am not sure about the retainer check, as we paid Gonzales $2000 by check that day.

The test was inconclusive. Zalud then asked for another $500 to send the document to Washington DC for more tests. The reason for all this was that Sessa was now claiming that the handwritten note was actually created after he had been told what we were claiming: he said he wrote down those figures in 1995, not 1992.

Thus was Zalud looking to prove otherwise. He may have also brought up Sessa's perjury of this during Sessa's deposition, I believe.

I was especially unhappy about the other $500 that I made out to Gonzales. If we could have gone to the feds to do it for that amount, why did we go to Gonzales in the first place?

Even after this, Elizabeth was sticking up for Zalud, saying such things as "Michael, give him a chance." But I was losing faith in him, and even though I tried not to show it, I believe Zalud could tell that I was.

We lunched with Zalud that day. We had lunched together at least three times before this, and I can't characterize any of these lunches as times when I showed my displeasure of Zalud's handling of our case.

I kept my feelings to myself.

February 23, 1996

Merrick's request for "Entire file for Escrow No. 16971" in preparation for a March 5 deposition.

— Was this for the deposition of Clement Morin? Or was it for Elizabeth's? I believe she gave hers before Sessa. She was the first one to be deposed.

February 26, 1996

Pauline Sessa's response to form interrogatories.

February 29, 1996

Deposition of Paolo Sessa, plus a letter dated ***April 11, 1996*** from Merrick to Zalud showing Sessa's correction to the text of his deposition.

— My wife and I were at this one. The deposition was held in Zalud's office. I remember feeling that Zalud was not asking Sessa what I would have asked him. Once or twice I even tried to interrupt him to point something out.

We went to lunch with Zalud this day, after the deposition. It seemed a pleasant enough lunch and, again, I kept my doubts about Zalud to myself. But I had tried to interrupt him while the deposition was going on, and I could tell he didn't like it.

After lunch, Zalud told us we didn't have to show up any more. From this point we stopped making our weekly trips to the courthouse, and we were not invited or even knew about Sessa's second deposition or any of the others that may have occurred. We only found out about them after the case was settled.

Obviously our relationship with Zalud was breaking down, and it may have begun with this deposition or the earlier event with Manny Gonzales. I remember not liking things, but I still didn't show it to him, not until after the case was all over.

Chapter 7
Zalud's Mantra

March 4, 1996

From Merrick: notice of deposition of Clement Morin.

Also, undated declaration of attorney N. Munro Merrick in support of deposition subpoena.

Also, proof of service by Joseph J. Strazzeri.

March 12, 1996

Letter from Joseph J. Strazzeri, Attorney at Law, to Zalud stating he recognizes the document as the agreement between the Ceperichs and Sessas.

— Strazzeri was Merrick's associate. We also showed Strazzeri the $900,000 note from Sessa. Zalud may have been trying to prove that the note existed before Sessa claims to have written it. I believe by this time that Zalud may have got back inconclusive results form DC as well, though he never said a word more to me about the results from DC.

March 19, 1996

Declaration of Kenneth J. Zalud in Opposition of Motion for Leave to File Amendment, with pages 110-11 & 92-94 attached.

March 20, 1996

Deposition of Clement W. Morin by Merrick, who made the point that the Ceperichs never claimed more than $500,000 as the selling price for the Park.

— But we did go to Morin later and revised our tax papers to show this, and we even paid the $24,000 in federal, $16,000 in state, $6,000 in county back taxes, and other losses—it came to nearly $60,000.

This was the figure that Merrick mentions at some point, and Zalud told me that I'd be getting this back from the government. Actually, I got back money from the county and a little from the state, but never the $24,000 we paid the feds.

On what legal precedence is this based? If it was appropriate, why didn't we get the federal tax money back, as well? Did Zalud fail us here, as well?

Moreover, since Morin can state that we paid the taxes, I can only suppose that Merrick was trying to prove that we were willing to pay $24,000 in order to perpetrate a ruse.

Also, it seems that Zalud should have tried somehow to get on the record that we'd paid the back taxes on the other $400,000 in early 1995. Of course, I wasn't included in any of these deliberations or I might have brought it up to my attorney. In fact, I didn't know that Morin had been deposed until after the case was over.

March/April, 1996

This was when we heard that we were not going to have a jury trial.

Also, soon after this occurred, Zalud visited us and told us that the judge wanted us to pay the taxes on one of Sessa's mobile homes, the one that the Park worker was living in. Zalud said that it amounted to $70 and that I had to pay it.

I didn't buy or own the mobile home and I didn't own the Park, so I didn't figure I had to pay taxes on Sessa's property. I told him I wouldn't pay it.

He then told me the judge would incarcerate me if I didn't pay the money, and Elizabeth broke down and cried.

Zalud then said that he'd pay the $70, but I said, "No, you're not. We'll pay it." And I told Elizabeth to write a check.

May 6, 1996

From Zalud to "Pauline Sessa and her attorney of record, N. Munro Merrick," Notice to Appear at Trial on ***May 31***; and another to Paolo Sessa.

— It's very possible that, since this occurred after Zalud told us not to show up any more, we weren't informed about this trial date. In any case, I don't recall a trial date being set at this time, nor whether there was one held.

May 30, 1996

From Zalud, Verified Answer to First Amendment to First Amended Complaint, drafted May 27.

July 19, 1996

Deposition of Pauline Sessa, by Zalud of Sachrison & Zalud; present was Zalud, Merrick, Strazzeri (Certified Student, PTLS), and Paolo Sessa.

— We weren't present, but according to the record, there seemed a heated debate between Zalud and Merrick. Apparently, Mrs. Sessa brought none of the asked-for documents concerning the running of the Park, the expenses, etc.

Could the short length of this deposition and the inability of Zalud to get the information from Mrs. Sessa show his failure in any way to represent us? I wish I had been there to actually see what was going on.

July 23, 1996

Deposition of Paolo Sessa (2nd) by Zalud, with Merrick and Pauline Sessa also present.

— Again, we were not there, but it seems to be an attempt to respond to Merrick going after Morin to document possible tax fraud by us not claiming more than $500,000 in capital gains, in that Zalud attacks Sessa's claim that the Park made no profit (110-11 in 2/26 deposition).

Merrick claimed that the improvements paid for though the Park account is not money out of Sessa's pocket.

Also, Zalud questioned Sessa about the property boundary and our walks around to the property markers, and about how he came to the monetary figures for damage due to losing two mobile home pads, and to lost business.

Sessa actually mentions that the tenants were complaining that the Park wasn't what it used to be. Imagine that: Sessa was now blaming us for his own mismanagement.

August 1, 1996

Damage assessment for Sessa, made by Appraisals Unlimited. It contains various photos of property and claims "damages sustained by the loss of 2 mobile home spaces as of October 30, 1992 to be: $103,000."

— Actually, if I had completed the road, which I didn't, Sessa would only have lost one mobile home pad—space #29. The other space, #30, was only in question because the tenants had illegally added a bedroom to the occupying mobile home which made it go past the original boundaries. This space could have been made legal and the mobile home pad not lost. We had nothing to do with this situation.

August 16, 1996

From Merrick, Notice to Compel Attendance at Trial and Bring Documents, for Ceperichs to appear on August 19, drafted by Merrick on July 29.

— The case was close to the end, and I was told by Zalud that I was going to be heard by the judge, finally.

August 30, 1996

List of trial exhibits.

Trial Briefs, both Zalud's and Merrick's.

— These are key documents of original arguments.

Chapter 8
Our Day in Court

September 3, 1996

Transcript of Settlement Hearing before Judge Hollywood.

— When asked by the judge if I agreed to the settlement, I answered obliquely, but I finally said yes, as I had been instructed to do by Zalud.

Zalud later used this in arbitration to argue that I had indeed had my day in court and could have said anything I wanted to the judge.

Chapter 9
Insult to Injury

November, 1996

Elizabeth and I were told by Zalud that we were going to see the judge and have our say. But the meeting was a joke.

Did Zalud set this up to placate me? In retrospect, it seems to me to be so, as Judge Hollywood never gave us the opportunity to state our case.

December 9, 1996

Letter from Spoon to Judge Hollywood: "The Ceperich's are to refund to the Sessa's $100,000 down payment plus $21,777 for the value of the various trailers, mobile homes, propane inventory and capital improvements."

— Sessa obviously made false statements to Spoon. There was only one trailer, since Sessa sold one of them in the interim, and one mobile home.

And this was the second accounting by Spoon. The first was also filled with lies by Sessa, but I haven't yet been able to get this document back from Zalud as he later promised at the arbitration hearing.

The mobile home was $4000 and the trailer was another $4000. He sold one other trailer for $1500, which would knock the figure down to $6500. As for the propane inventory, I had to eventually pay off the outstanding bill on the propane. And it cost me my good relationship with my propane dealer.

Not to mention that, by agreement, he wasn't to sell any of the property of the Park, and he did. The list of things that Sessa disposed of includes the antique truck, the trailer that the Park worker was living in, the gas motor for the shredder, and various other items that belonged to the Park.

He didn't sell the backhoe, but he ruined it.

Late 1996/Early 1997

From Merrick: Memorandum of Points and Authorities in Support of Motion for Judgment of Rescission, with a "Net adjusted total due the Sessas... of $228,165."

— It is peculiar that the stamped file date seems to have been cut out, and it's not dated at the end of the document as is typical.

Also, during this time Zalud was slowly forcing me to give in to the Judge's stipulation to pay Sessa some money for compensation. I had refused the over $200,000 figure. Our relationship with Zalud hit an all-time low, maybe with me more than Elizabeth still, but she was heartbroken at this time. She would say often, "Why did we ever meet these people?"

January 24, 1997

Hearing paper showing Judge H.R. Hollywood's breakdown of moneys and order for the Ceperichs "to pay the Sessas the amount of $170,537."

Also, drafted January 17 by Merrick, Memorandum of Points and Authorities in Reply to Defendants' Memorandum. It concludes: "the goal of recision is to restore both parties to their former position as far as possible."

— But it didn't return me to my former position as far as possible. I wanted a strait recision since it was Sessa who was breaking the contract. I don't believe I should have paid Sessa anything. Even then, I'd have still lost on the deal, especially since the profit claimed by Sessa—$17,400—was considerably lower than what I would have made owning the Park.

Indeed, $100,000 per year for four years equals $400,000. Of the $9000 a month that Sessa pulled in, he paid me approximately $5000 per month, which leaves nearly $200,000 in profit that Sessa disposed of somehow, but that I would have had use of as profit had I owned the Park.

At some point Zalud said to me, "Oh, we got him!" and told me that Sessa admitted that he'd made $174,000 in profit owning the Park. But this happened after I was forced to agree to pay Sessa $160,000 to get back the Park.

I'm not sure what good this was to know at this point in the proceedings. It should have been brought up before Judge Hollywood made his stipulation and I had to agree to pay Sessa for the Park, even though it was Sessa who had defaulted on our agreement, not me.

Zalud's mantras of "We got him" and " Got your Park back" rang hollow in the end. I now feel Zalud was only placating us with his words, maybe just to get the case over with. Regardless, was justice served? I believe not.

January 27, 1997

Building plan for the garage for our modular home approved. Fire Marshal inspection signed off.

February 11, 1997

County building inspector correction report for garage.

March 1, 1997

Called District Attorney, Anthony Samram.

— I was still trying to get hold of DA Pfingst. It was unbelievable to us that Pfingst wouldn't be interested in our case, as he'd made such a big deal on the television about going after senior fraud cases and ours was that.

Apparently, our case was not big enough to warrant the district attorney's attention. Or, possibly, Pfingst's office did look into it in an exploratory fashion and decided our situation was not suitable to his political ends. I wish I knew the answer to this.

Regardless, we were very disappointed at Pfingst's lack of response.

March 4, 1997

Inspection of siding for garage.

March 11, 1997

Stipulation for Judgment

Pauline Sessa

Elizabeth Marie Ceperich

N. Munro Merrick
Attorney for Plaintiffs

Kenneth Zalud
Attorney for Defendants

Joseph J. Strazzeri
Attorney for Plaintiffs

ORDER

On reading and filing the agreement and stipulation of the parties hereto for entry of judgment herein, and good cause appearing therefor,

IT IS HEREBY ORDERED that judgment be entered as follows:

1. The parties agree and declare that the contract between Plaintiffs and Defendants for the sale of the Ramona Mobile Park, together with all promissory notes and other associated obligations, has been rescinded;

2. Defendants shall pay Plaintiff within sixty (60) days form this date the sum of $160,000.00, together with interest thereon at the rate of ten percent per annum, interest to accrue beginning sixty days from the date of this stipulation;

3. Plaintiff is ordered to transfer title and possession of the Park, excluding a certain mobilehome (Decal Lat9544) occupied by Martin Estrada (the Estrada Mobilehome), to Defendants on condition that Defendants pay to Plaintiffs the sum ordered by this judgment;

4. Plaintiff shall have 90 days (the Removal Period) from date of judgment to remove the Estrada Mobilehome. During that period of time plaintiff, his agents, prospective purchasers and real estate personnel (Authorized Persons) shall have unrestricted access to the park and the Estrada Mobilehome for any purpose reasonably connected with the sale and/or removal of the mobilehome, and Defendants, their agents and associates shall not impede access to the mobilehome by any Authorized

Second page of Stipulation for Judgment:

Person, in any manner, or talk to anyone coming on the property for purposes authorized by this stipulation except to identify the visitor as an Authorized Person.

Each party affirms that s/he has reviewed the terms of this stipulation, that s/he understands each and every term and condition, that s/he has consulted with his/her attorney of choice and has discussed this stipulation with said attorney, that s/he agrees to each and every term and condition, agrees to do nothing to impede or hinder the performance of this agreement, and promises to take whatever actions are necessary to assure the faithful performance of all his/her obligations under this agreement.

Should any action or proceeding be necessary to enforce the provisions of this settlement agreement, the prevailing party shall be entitled to recovery of all his/her costs including reasonable attorneys' fees.

— What's interesting here is that I took from this document that I wasn't to talk to anyone, which is a hard way to conduct business. Indeed, for a while I was afraid to talk to anyone at the Park.

March 13, 1997

Abstract of Judgment.

— As I've said, I'd have been happy with just getting the Park back because Sessa defaulted on our agreement, but, instead, I actually had to pay him for the time he ran the Park. This was an outrage as far as I was concerned. Sessa was allowed $1000 a month for running the Park.

March 18, 1997

Letter from Zalud to Merrick arguing that the lien placed on the Ceperichs will only hinder them getting the $160,000 and complaining of Merrick's use of "obscenities in referring to [his] client."

— At first I saw this document as an indictment of attorneys generally and how rude and ungentlemanly they can be. And it is that. But I now see it also as Zalud placating me.

March 24, 1997

Letter from Zalud to Clem Morin stating FYI that Sessa was paid $45,000 "for the value of his time running the Park (management fee- $30,000) and reasonable return on the $100,000 down payment ($15,000)."

— This was the offset for the "$45,000 in unreported income" that Sessa made while owning the Park.

This seems to be saying that Sessa was covered for the unreported income, but why would they do this? Again, let me say that I had to pay him for the return of my Park.

Also, as I've said, I'd have been happy just to get the Park back without having to pay Sessa anything, but I believe that had I wanted to make an issue of it or, rather, if Zalud had, a strong case could be made that Sessa should have to pay me for the interest on the unpaid $100,000 and for the time I put in running the Park for him.

Ultimately, we paid over $200,000 for the return of our property. This includes getting no interest on the second $100,000 out-of-escrow payment and no payment for the 18 months that we actually managed the Park for the Sessas, not to mention that Sessa never showed the profit that he must have made with the Park.

I couldn't believe that I was going to be forced to pay Sessa anything. I was completely despondent about not being heard in court and unhappy with our attorney for dropping the ball.

After I refused the nearly $300,000 figure, Zalud came back with an offer of a little over $200,000, which I also refused.

"Mike," said Zalud, "if you don't agree, the judge will go back to $282,000."

In retrospect, I see that Zalud was doing his best to scare us into the agreement. This occurred over the course of a few weeks. The next time we saw Zalud, he gave us the final offer of $160,000.

I was still inclined not to take it for the reasons I've already stated, but Elizabeth was not well, and we were eager to put this behind us. Indeed, the ordeal was taking its toll on both of us. We'd aged more in those few years than in the 50 or so of our life together before Sessa walked into it.

April 2, 1997

First bill from Zalud for $22,868.

— I didn't immediately pay this bill as I was angry about our representation by Zalud. Besides, I was preoccupied with my concern over Elizabeth's health, so I had a lot on my mind otherwise.

Moreover, I eventually realized just how much was going on that I didn't know about. All the depositions, forensic accountings and negotiations over settlement figures—all important events in the proceedings, and I was privy to none of them.

April 21, 1997

Final inspection for garage.

May 11, 1997

Notice from Sessa raising the rent on space #18 to $5000 per month.

May 13, 1997

Elizabeth Marie Ceperich
Michael Mark Ceperich
2020 Orange Avenue
Ramona CA 92065

Dear Mr. and Mrs. Ceperich:

You are hereby notified that the rent on the premises currently occupied by you at the Ramona Mobilehome Park, 2030 BlackCanyon Road in Ramona, will be increased to $5000.00 per month effective June 16, 1997. The rental payment in that amount will be due and payable on or before June 16, 1997.

If you fail to pay the rent on or before that date, legal proceedings will be commenced immediately against you for possession of the premises, and damages for unlawfully detaining the property will be $166.67 per day.

Very truly yours,

Paolo Sessa

— Since the final judgment had already been made and the Park was about to be turned over to us again, this was a vicious ploy on Sessa's part to bring my wife and me more pain than he had already inflicted. He was obviously uncaring at best about ruining our health, two retired people in our late 70s.

Of course, these obvious distortions and lies and unfair actions had to become obvious to his attorneys, and he was forced from time to time to change his council. By the time he wrote the above letter to us, he was on his third different attorney.

May 13, 1997

Both an eviction notice (30 days) and another outrageous letter from Sessa raising our rent to $5000 per month to begin June 16.

Also, from Merrick, a one-page Writ of Execution (Money Judgment) showing $160,000 figure. This goes with levy of garnishment to pay Sessas.

Also from Merrick, an Abstract of Judgment.

— Interesting that Walters and Ward were named along with Elizabeth and me in the Information on Additional Debtors. It seems that the Sessas were in debt to their attorneys, as well, or at least at odds with their previous attorneys.

But more: Since Sessa was about to return the Park to us officially, this eviction notice seemed to have little to do with anything except to harass two elderly people, my wife and me. To the end, Sessa, the same man who used to kiss me on the cheek, was vindictive and hurtful.

May 18, 1997

Letter from County Assessor's Office enclosing Notice of Involuntary Lien against the Park.

— This was another harassing ploy by Sessa.

May 20, 1997

Substitution of attorney, from N. Munro Merrick to Joseph J. Strazzeri.

Also, notice to appear for Ceperichs, something to do with capability to pay debt to Sessas.

Also, order to Show Cause why Ceperichs haven't yet paid Sessas for return of Park.

— Again, these actions were nothing more than harassment by the Sessas and their attorneys. I did feel it was unfair to have to pay them anything, but the reason I hadn't was that we didn't have the money and would have to borrow it.

May/June, 1997

It was around this time that we were to meet with the Sessas and our attorneys at the Park to make sure that they left behind all that belonged to the Park. But by the time we got there, which was at least ten minutes before the appointed time, the Sessas had already packed everything and our attorney was conversing casually with their attorney, Strazzeri.

Also, Sessa actually took all the papers for the Park, including all of mine from the time we owned the Park and all those we had kept of the Mersmans, who owned it before us, and of the Dukes, who owned it before them. All these papers were taken by Sessa—illegally, as the judge had stipulated that all documents of the Park should stay with the Park.

Sessa also took the current leases which showed who had paid what and how much, deposits and closing rents, etc. We had to ask Zalud to get back the long-term leases for the tenants. Zalud first told us that Sessa claimed he didn't have them, but then, about a month later, Zalud told us that he had got them back and we had them again.

But these were the only papers we got back. All the others, including renters' applications and other signed legal documents, we never saw again.

After this, even Elizabeth was disappointed with Zalud and showed it. After we picked up the final papers from Zalud, she broke down and cried.

Chapter 10
Dissolution

May 27, 1997

Two letters asking for help, one to Hunter and one to Bilbray, mentioning DA Pfingst's TV appearance.

May 28, 1997

We retained Robert W. Zickert to get justice. After what happened with all the Park papers and any item that was not nailed down being already loaded in the Sessas' cars, and my attorney talking and laughing with Sessa's attorney while I stood there helplessly, I told Zalud that he was colluding. He dropped me like a hot potato after that.

May 30, 1997

Another letter to Duncan Hunter.

I hope you will be victorious in Court!!
Valerie

VALERIE SNESKO
Office Manager
366 South Pierce Street
El Cajon, CA 92020
(619) 579-3001
Fax (619) 579-2251
Ramona (619) 788-3630

Duncan Hunter
Member of Congress
52nd District, California

...use of Representatives
...gton, DC 20515-0552

2265 Rayburn Building
Washington, DC 20515-0552
(202) 225-5672
Fax (202) 225-0235

366 South Pierce Street
El Cajon, CA 92020
(619) 579-3001

1101 Airport Road, Suite G
Imperial, CA 92251
(619) 353-5420

1410 Main Street, Suite C
Ramona, CA 92065
(619) 788-3630

May 30, 1997

Mr. & Mrs. Michael Ceperich
2020 Orange Avenue
Ramona, CA 92065

Dear Mr. & Mrs. Ceperich:

Thank you for your recent letter to my office requesting assistance with your current situation. I can understand your problem and would like very much to be of assistance to you. Unfortunately, your circumstance involves the court and I am unable to be of service in this area.

I have forwarded your letter to District Attorney, Paul Pfingst. I am sure you will be hearing from him shortly.

In the meantime, thank you for thinking of me and be assured of my continuing interest in your problem.

Sincerely,

Duncan Hunter

Duncan Hunter
Member of Congress

DH/vs

And the response from Hunter's office.

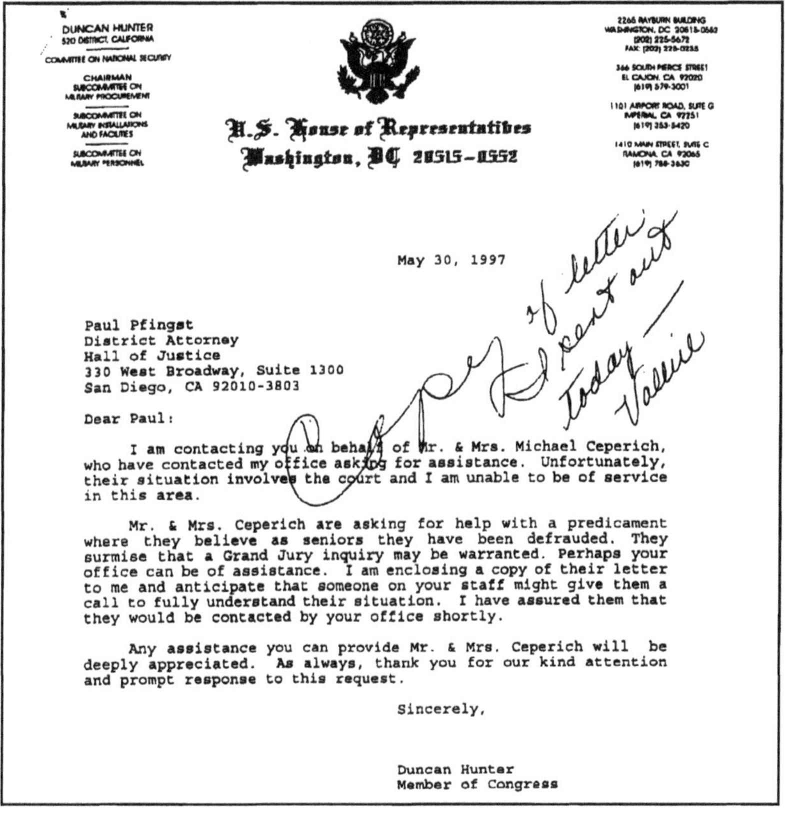

DUNCAN HUNTER
52D DISTRICT, CALIFORNIA

COMMITTEE ON NATIONAL SECURITY

CHAIRMAN
SUBCOMMITTEE ON
MILITARY PROCUREMENT

SUBCOMMITTEE ON
MILITARY INSTALLATIONS
AND FACILITIES

SUBCOMMITTEE ON
MILITARY PERSONNEL

U.S. House of Representatives
Washington, DC 20515–0552

2265 RAYBURN BUILDING
WASHINGTON, DC 20515-0552
(202) 225-5672
FAX: (202) 225-0235

366 SOUTH PIERCE STREET
EL CAJON, CA 92020
(619) 579-3001

1101 AIRPORT ROAD, SUITE G
IMPERIAL, CA 92251
(619) 353-5420

1410 MAIN STREET, SUITE C
RAMONA, CA 92065
(619) 788-3630

May 30, 1997

Copy of letter I sent out today — Valerie

Paul Pfingst
District Attorney
Hall of Justice
330 West Broadway, Suite 1300
San Diego, CA 92010-3803

Dear Paul:

I am contacting you on behalf of Mr. & Mrs. Michael Ceperich, who have contacted my office asking for assistance. Unfortunately, their situation involves the court and I am unable to be of service in this area.

Mr. & Mrs. Ceperich are asking for help with a predicament where they believe as seniors they have been defrauded. They surmise that a Grand Jury inquiry may be warranted. Perhaps your office can be of assistance. I am enclosing a copy of their letter to me and anticipate that someone on your staff might give them a call to fully understand their situation. I have assured them that they would be contacted by your office shortly.

Any assistance you can provide Mr. & Mrs. Ceperich will be deeply appreciated. As always, thank you for our kind attention and prompt response to this request.

Sincerely,

Duncan Hunter
Member of Congress

June 2, 1997

Letter from Brian Bilbray stating that Mike's letter for help was being forwarded to Congressman Duncan Hunter.

June 6, 1997

Sessa through some company named Douglas J. Goodman accessed Mike's credit report.

Also, sample form letter from Strazzeri to Zickert and to be sent to tenants concerning garnishment instructions.

— Around this time, one of the tenants, Pearson Bickel, told me that he had a lease, as did other renters, papers which I did not have as Sessa had taken all the papers with him.

Eventually, Zalud brought me the leases for my renters. He evidently got them from Sessa, after a period of over a month.

June 13, 1997

Change of Attorney to Robert W. Zickert.

— I told Zickert about not being represented properly by Zalud, among other things, and he agreed that it seemed that it was so. But he advised against pursuing a claim of a mistrial or to appeal the judgment.

Zickert did admit to me that he thought we had been misrepresented by Zalud and that he could have helped us better if he had had the case from the start.

Also, Zickert's Attorney Retainer Agreement—$5000.

Also, letter from Zickert to Spoon enclosing check for $2,351.64 from Ceperichs, their half of court appointed accountant fees which were in arrears.

— I still don't have the forensic accountant's report. As I've said, Zalud never gave them to me and Spoon cannot give them to me without an attorney's official query. So I paid this money to Spoon's firm, but have no right to the documents?

June 16,1997

Letter to *San Diego Union Tribune* (hard to read as it's a faded copy of the original). Sent also to DA Pfingst and to Judge Hollywood.

— It stated something to the extent that Sessa has more power than the judge. I was referring mostly to the incident at the Park when the Sessas absconded with all the important Park papers, both current and from the past, and my attorney at the time didn't seem interested to help at all with it.

June 17, 1997

From law office of Robert W. Zickert to Mrs. Ceperich enclosing a "copy of the Stipulation for Entry of Judgment and Order as you requested."

Also, Order to Show Cause why Ceperichs haven't paid Sessas and to appear in court before Judge Hollywood.

Also, Declaration of Robert W. Zickert Re Order to Show Cause for Nonpayment of Court Ordered Accounting Fees.

— The pressure was on for us to pay Sessa his money, I suspect because others, such as Sessa's previous attorneys, had an interest in getting paid through Sessa's settlement with me.

June 18, 1997

Letter from Joseph J. Strazzeri (formerly with Law Offices of N. Munro Merrick) to Pearson Bickel, renter at RMHP, explaining "the Memorandum of Garnishee that has been served on" him, to be paid until the $160,000 owed the Sessas for the return of RMHP to the Ceperichs.

— We were still working on the loan, but I guess it wasn't happening fast enough for all concerned. Thus the lien.

June 20, 1997

Letter from Zickert to Ceperichs clarifying that all payments by tenants were to go to Sessa's $160,000 lien, but a loan from Great Western Bank was looking good.

Also, letter from Zickert to Strazzeri explaining and straightening things out.

Also, undated (but received June 23) letter to Zickert from Elizabeth enclosing a court letter and informing of meeting with Charlotte Buse from Grossmont Bank.

June 25, 1997

Letter from Strazzeri to Zickert claiming that judgment was in favor of his clients, the Sessas, and including a copy of the Stipulation for Judgment.

— This contradicts Zalud's claim that he won the case for us. At this point, Zickert was doing well for us, but the case was already over, and there was little he could do about changing the results. I do, indeed, wish that we had had him from the start.

Also, letter from Zickert to Strazzeri enclosing two checks from tenants Brenner and Tupper.

Also, Judgment Debtor's Exam postponed from July 3 to August 8.

June 30, 1997

Letter from tenant Juanita Parnell to Marshall of SD County stating that last month's rent to be withheld due to paying it to Sessa when she moved in.

— She asked me for the money and I told her that I didn't have any of the money that Sessa had collected, and she then called Strazzeri and argued her case. Later Strazzeri sent me a letter charging me $17.50 for his time talking to Ms. Parnell!

I assume he took it out of the lien money he was collecting from the tenants. Just one more person feeding off of the situation. It seemed nobody would be excluded from benefiting.

Later in 98-99, another tenant, Mary Koppel asked me for her last month's rent. Actually, this is when I found out that Sessa had done this with everybody at the Park. Before this, I thought it was just something he did with Ms. Parnell, but Sessa had done it with all the new tenants.

July 9, 1997

Letter from Zickert notifying Ceperichs of above rescheduling and enclosing Brenner's check. States that involuntary lien will be removed once judgment is settled.

July 15, 1997

Letter from Elizabeth to Zickert enclosing three checks from tenants and a letter dated July 3 from tenant Brenda Boggus.

— Since we collected the rent from some tenants, we had to forward the checks to Zickert. Later, all of them were sent straight to the Marshall by the tenants.

July 17, 1997

Letter from Zickert to Strazzeri enclosing Boggus and Tupper checks and asking for preliminary accounting.

— I had never gotten the accounting from Zalud.

July 29, 1997

Letter from Strazzeri to Zickert showing a preliminary accounting, March through July, of the $160,000 judgment with added fees and interest and subtracted payments from tenants.

— How accurate this accounting is I have no idea, as they never shared with me any of the figures.

August 1, 1997

Letter from Zickert to Strazzeri enclosing new date of Debtor's Exam, originally July 3, from August 8 to August 22.

Also letter from Zickert stating that Ceperich's loan from Charlotte at Grossmont Bank has been approved and enclosing Strazzeri's preliminary accounting. Says will talk on Monday, August 4, about preliminary accounting and "final payoff" figure.

August 4, 1997

Letter from Zickert restating the above and strongly advising a title search to make sure Sessas didn't encumber the property.

August 6, 1997

Letter from Zickert to Strazzeri stating that Charlotte at Grossmont Bank is to process a check to the Sessas and Strazzeri in amount of $154,465.31, and enclosing a proposed grant deed, an Acknowledgment of Satisfaction of Judgment, and a copy of the letter to tenants informing them of the change.

Also, five-page Release & Settlement Agreement between Walters & Ward and the Sessas.

— Evidently Walters & Ward were the defendants, sued for professional negligence, breach of fiduciary duty, and breach of contract. But the Sessas paid them $15,000 in attorney's fees as part of settlement.

August 7, 1997

Letter from Strazzeri to Zickert responding to Zickert's August 1 letter to Strazzeri.

August 11, 1997

Letter from Zickert to Ceperichs outlining the status of the matter, including the final settlement figure of $154,465 and stating that the Ceperichs did not want to expend $1000-2100 for a title search, but Zickert did a rudimentary search on August 7 and found the following:

November 27, 1973—grant deed from Clarence Dukes to Michael and Elizabeth Ceperich; October 11, 1991—from Ceperichs as individuals to Ceperich trust; October 16, 1992—from Ceperich Trust to Paolo and Pauline Sessa.

— Zickert was to meet with the Sessas and their attorney and Charlotte of Grossmont Bank on August 14 to conclude the transaction.

August 14, 1997

Grant Deed from Sessa to Ceperichs.

Acknowledgment of Satisfaction of Judgment.

Letter to tenants to start paying Ceperichs again.

Letter from Zickert to Strazzeri to sign and forward any further checks received from Marshall's Office to Zickert.

— We were both quite disillusioned at this time. Elizabeth had given up trying to make any sense of it, and she even refused to be home when Zalud and Strazzeri visited to debate how Sessa was losing money on an electrical rebate.

August 18,1997

Letter from Zickert to Ceperichs indicating the above exchanges.

— He also states that Strazzeri's argument is that the condition of the back hoe was taken into account by the $160,000 settlement figure, and he doesn't feel it would be in the Ceperich's best interest to pursue a separate lawsuit about it.

Also, a letter from Strazzeri to Zickert enclosing a check from the Marshall's Office and a copy of a letter to Barbara at the Marshall's Office to send all further checks to Zickert.

Also, letter from Elizabeth to Zickert about taxes due on trailers and the many missing things Mike was finding: a kerosene heater, typewriter, chain saw, cutoff saw, and shredder, and the condition of the backhoe, etc.

August 19, 1997

Letter from Strazzeri to Zickert enclosing another check from Marshall's Office.

— The checks that were going straight to Strazzeri after the lien now had to be rerouted back to us.

August 27, 1997

Letter from Zickert to tenant Jim Coleman confirming his agreement to pay three-month's back rent and move his trailer by September 10.

Also, letter from Fidelity National Title enclosing a Change of Ownership to be filled out and returned.

September 2, 1997

Letter from Zickert enclosing another check from the Marshall's Office for $5393.50.

September 4, 1997

Letter from Strazzeri to Zickert enclosing a check from the Marshall's Office for $310.

September 10, 1997

Letter from Zickert enclosing a copy of Grant Deed and Preliminary Change of Ownership filed on September 3 and two more checks

September 12, 1997

Letter from Strazzeri to Zickert enclosing check for $310.

September 15, 1997

Letter from Zickert enclosing last check from Strazzeri and concluding his relationship with Ceperichs. His final bill to follow.

September 19, 1997

Letter from Jeffrey Brodick, Deputy District Attorney, congratulating Mike for getting a favorable settlement against Sessa.

— So they finally responded to our letters, after the fact. And, as I've said, I don't consider the settlement in our favor. Funny that both our attorney and Sessa's were claiming victory.

As Zalud's chorus went, "You got your Park back!"

And as mine has been, "Yes, but at what cost?"

September 25, 1997

Letter from SD Bar, Client Relations Committee Informal Complaints, stating Mike's complaint "is beyond the scope of [their] activities" and suggesting that Mike contact the State Bar of California.

— This is in response to our complaint against Zalud. Even though Zickert had advised us against suing Zalud, we decided to pursue some action against him, even if it was just to complain to the Bar.

Elizabeth was not surprised at this response, as she had suggested when we sent the letter that we'd just be bucking the system. She was right.

October 6, 1997

Letter to State Bar (runaround?)

Also, a letter from Zickert enclosing a copy of the Acknowledge of Satisfaction of Judgment, recorded on August 18, 1997.

October 31, 1997

Letter from Bar stating that "errors in judgment and mere negligence, by an attorney, do not form the basis for disciplinary action by the State Bar"

— This was signed by Teresa Osante, Complaint Analyst.

December 25, 1997

We broke the ice and gave each other gifts again.

April 3, 1998

Forms from California Bar.

July 6, 1998

Same bill from Zalud for $22,868.

June 10, 1998

From Zalud: "Notice of Client's Right to Arbitration"

July 10, 1998

Letter from SD County Bar Association approving reduction for filing fee re Zalud arbitration.

August 28, 1998

Elizabeth passed away. She died brokenhearted and disappointed. She had lost the will to live.

Chapter 11
Zalud's Revenge

October 8, 1998

Same bill from Zalud for $22,868.

— At some point Zalud offered to settle for $15,000 and I offered him $10,000. This occurred over the phone. He refused. The whole conversation was short.

April 1, 1999

Same bill from Zalud for $22,868.

April 5, 1999

Arbitration notice: Mike applicant, Zalud respondent.

— In essence, I didn't really apply for arbitration, but was more like pushed into it.

April 29, 1999

A letter from Lewis, D'Amato, Brisbois & Bisgaard, who conducted the arbitration for the Bar.

— They also asked me if I wanted to add any documents or materials to the arbitration panel, and three documents submitted by Zalud were enclosed:

1) Transcript of settlement hearing on September 3, 1996, at which Ceperichs were present; 2) Report by Roberta Spoon to Judge Hollywood dated December 9, 1996; 3) Stipulation for Entry of Judgment and Order filed March 11, 1997.

June 21, 1999

Letter from SD County Bar enclosing Arbitration Findings and Award, among other documents, such as Mike's application for arbitration dated ***July 6, 1998*** and a five-page letter from Brodshatzer, Wallace, Spoon & Yip, accountants, to Judge Hollywood recommending the Sessas be repaid their $100,000 down payment "plus $21,777 for the value of the various trailers, mobile homes, propane inventory and capital improvements" which was dated ***December 9, 1996***.

— Of course, I contest these figures, but I should have done so when Zalud came to us with the $160,000 figure, and I would have if I'd had a breakdown of the figures at that point. But, instead, we just had Zalud throwing settlement figures at us. As I've said, it seems obvious to me now that he only wanted us to settle, at any figure, regardless of fairness.

November 23, 1999

Order to Confirm Arbitration Award and for Entry of Judgment Thereon.

Also, Findings and Award from May 1999.

— I wasn't present at this meeting. I called two weeks ahead of time to change the date and was told that I should call back a couple of days before, which I did. At that time I was told that it was too late to change the date. I had again been taken advantage of. And I wouldn't get the opportunity to ask once more for the papers that Zalud still had.

If asked, I do remember the man's first name. It was Steve who told me to call back a couple of days before the scheduled date in order to change it, and then when I called back two days before, he told me it was too late.

Regardless, I didn't blame this person at the time. By then I was used to feeling that the cards were stacked against me and I accepted it as the norm, though I did decide to contact the State Bar again concerning Zalud.

December 10, 1999

I wrote the following letter to the State Bar:

State Bar of California
1149 South Hill Street
Los Angeles, CA 90015

December 10, 1999

Dear Madam,

As you requested when we talked on the phone, I am sending you this letter regarding my experiences with Mr. Kenneth Zalud and his representation of my case against Mr. Paolo Sessa, who bought Ramona Mobile Park from my wife and me in 1992 for $900,000—$400,000 of which was to be paid to a blind trust.

1. Mr. Zalud promised us a jury trial, but on the week a jury was to be selected, it was changed to a trial by judge, a Judge H. Hollywood. Zalud told us the judge had done this to save us money. On the day of this so-called trial, my wife and I sat in an empty room by ourselves. Judge Hollywood entered the room by himself, asked me if I'd ever been in court before, gruffly cut me off before I could ask what was going on and he stood up and left the room. My wife and I were again alone in the room for about 25 minutes more

until Zalud entered and told us it was over and we could leave. He never explained to us what happened, but we certainly didn't have our day in court.

2. When we asked him about the status of our valid contract with Mr. Sessa for the $400,000 blind trust, Mr. Zalud told us that the judge didn't see it as valid. Again it seemed unbelievable to us as the document had already been proclaimed valid in a previous judgment in our favor against Mr. Sessa.

3. Mr. Zalud told us not to cash nearly $34,000 of checks given to us by Mr. Sessa as payment for Ramona Mobile Park. Zalud told us to keep them uncashed as evidence. Eventually he told us that Judge Hollywood wanted to see the checks, so we surrendered them to Zalud. We made copies of the checks, but we were never given a receipt for them by Zalud. That was the last we ever saw of those checks. To this day, I have no idea if they were ever cashed.

4. Mr. Zalud told me that the judge ruled that we had to pay the taxes on a mobile home bought by Sessa when he was the owner of the Mobile Park. Again we did what we were told even though it seemed to make no sense.

There are many other things that I could mention to show how my now deceased wife and I were taken advantage of by Mr. Zalud, how we were given wrong or contradicting information by him and how he has since refused to return to me the many important documents that he still has of mine. I am 83 years old and writing is difficult for me, but I would be willing to give you more of the details on the phone.

Sincerely,
Michael M. Ceperich

January 18, 2000

Letter to AARP for help finding an attorney.

January 24, 2000

Notice of Levy—Garnishment, from San Diego County Marshal.

— Now it was Zalud's turn.

Chapter 12
Final Appeal

March 27, 2000

Despairing letter to Congressman Hunter, via Mr. Cedillo.

— Cato Cedillo was deputy chief of staff for congressman Hunter.

April 17, 2000

Letter from Bar to Mike explaining that they cannot take action against Zalud and enclosing a previous letter to Mike dated October 31, 1997, stating basically the same, as both of Mike's complaints were the same against Zalud; in other words, no new evidence was brought forth.

April 24, 2000

Letter from Mike to new attorney, Eugene P. Yale, showing proof of payment to attorney Zickert and enclosing the April 28 letter that Mike received from the Ramona law offices of Krysak & McNicol concerning payment of utilities.

Also, a San Diego Superior Court Records Request form and receipt to Amber Yale dated April 19.

May 4, 2000

Forwarded to Yale by Mike, a questionnaire dated April 26 from the Lawyer Referral & Information Service concerning participating attorney, Mr. C. Dan Conaway.

— I was reaching out to everyone I could for help. I got this attorney's name from the AARP. I explained to him my situation with Zalud, and he told me to pay him and get on with my life.

May 5, 2000

Letter from Yale to Zalud stating that Zalud did a poor job of representation: Zalud failed to pursue the fraud aspect, which if he had would have resulted in the Ceperichs not have to pay for improvements to the Park or to the Sessas for managing the Park or even probably the $100,000 down payment.

"Instead, the Ceperichs had to pay $160,000 to the people who defrauded them, and, according to you have spent/will spend over $40,000 for your services. Thus, the Ceperichs, who owned the property for about thirty years, lost over $100,000 in rents (the difference between the rents received by the fraudmakers and the payments on the promissory notes), incurred over $40,000 in attorneys' fees, and had to pay more than $60,000 out of pocket to the people who cheated them. That is not a good result. What is especially egregious in this case is that you had the fraud in writing (the *unsecured, NO INTEREST* $400,000 promissory note), you had an unenforceable *oral* sale of real property, and you had the presumption of "Slick Willy" taking undue advantage of senior citizens, fleecing them out of their property they had owned for thirty years. And, to add insult to injury, the fraudmakers had the audacity to sue the Ceperichs to specifically enforce the fraudulently induced agreement."

Also, a letter from Zalud to Yale defending his representation of the Ceperichs.

May 9, 2000

Letter from Yale to Zalud confirming "an ex-parte hearing for ... May 11."

May 10, 2000

Ex-parte application to set aside judgment on Zalud.

Also, a Declaration of Eugene P. Yale, including that Zalud refused to provide him with Ceperich's paperwork. He goes on to state that Zalud served his motion 14 days before the hearing, when 15 days is required by law.

Also, a copy of service proving 14 days and a letter to Zalud stating the inappropriateness.

Also, a letter from Zalud stating that not less than 10 days notice is needed, not 15.

Also, another letter from Zalud to Yale defending his position concerning Mike. Zalud states that Mike is not a newcomer to the business world and has enough experience to get things right as far as making appearances in court and time limits to appeal.

— But I *was* inexperienced in the world of lawsuits, so did he mean my experience with him, or with Sessa, or with Judge Hollywood?

All that these experiences did was to make me feel like a small animal caught paralyzed in the lights of an onrushing truck. I felt helpless to act, and Zalud took advantage of my helplessness.

May 11, 2000

Letter from Yale to Zalud informing that this day's ex-parte hearing has been postponed.

May 12, 2000

Yale's handwritten notes of Mike's interview.

Letter from Yale to Zickert asking for files.

May 13, 2000

Letter from Mike to Yale with photocopy of $5000 check to Zickert.

Also, undated various cases dealing with relief from judgments annotated by Yale.

May 16, 2000

Letter from Yale confirming that he wasn't going to file a motion to set aside Zalud's judgment against Mike because there is proof that Mike got the Arbitration Award papers; Yale agrees to help Mike recover $5000 from Attorney Krysak and write "a letter to the District Attorney regarding a potential perjury action against Mr. Sessma [sic]."

— I'm not sure what the $5000 figure is all about, unless Yale meant to say Zickert instead of Krysak. Regardless, I have no complaint with either Zickert or Krysak.

May 18, 2000

Letter from Yale to Zalud enclosing Ceperich's authorization to release his complete files to Yale's office.

May 19, 2000

Letter from Yale to Zickert to help find the Ceperich files.

May 22, 2000

Letter from Zickert to Yale expressing difficulty finding Ceperich file.

May 24, 2000

Yale's change of address

May 26, 2000

Letter from Zickert to Yale, answering Yale's May 12 letter and enclosing my authorization and the "original file related to the matter on which [he] assisted Mr. and Mrs. Ceperich."

Included is a bound file called "Pleadings," a chronological list of the key court proceedings and judgments.

— This was in one of two large envelopes of material from Zickert to Yale. Following is the table of contents and dates:

Pleadings

1.	Trial Briefs	8/30/96
2.	Accountants Report	12/9/96
3.	Stipulated Judgment	3/11/97
4.	Abstract of Judgment	5/13/97
5.	30 Day Notice to Quit	5/13/97
6.	Writ of Execution	5/13/97
7.	Judgment Debtors Exam	5/20/97
8.	Order to Show Cause	5/20/97

9. Substitution of Attorneys Forms 6/13/97
10. Declaration RWZ 6/13/97
11. Order to Show Cause 6/23/97
12. Change of Address 6/30/97
13. Notice of Entry of Judgment 6/30/97

February 6, 2001

Second letter from Yale to Zalud requesting an accounting of funds received from his levy and a Full Satisfaction on Judgment.

— Yale asked Zalud for this almost a year earlier on June 16, 2000. To this day, I still don't have the accounting, and Zalud's name still appears as lien holder on the Park.

Also, a letter from Yale to Roberta Spoon asking for the documents that Zalud never returned to me.

— To this day, I still don't have these documents.

About the Author

Michael Ceperich was born in 1916 in Steelton, Pennsylvania, the son of European immigrants. He went to high school in Steelton and attended Armour Institute of Technology in Chicago. He married Elizabeth Klein in 1940.

After spending two years, 1943-45, in the South Pacific as a member of the United States Navy, Mr. Ceperich worked as a production line designer/engineer for a food processing company and later for various oil and chemical companies.

A lifetime of hard work and saving culminated in his purchase in 1969 of a 35-space Mobile Home Park in Ramona, California.

Mr. Ceperich still resides in Ramona with his late wife's cat, Mascot.

www.ingramcontent.com/pod-product-compliance
Ingram Content Group UK Ltd.
Pitfield, Milton Keynes, MK11 3LW, UK
UKHW041847190726
13854UKWH00002B/753